NEVERLAND

OMNIBUS PRESS

LONDON / NEW YORK / PARIS / SYDNEY / COPENHAGEN / BERLIN / MADRID / HONG KONG / TOKYO

Copyright © 2012 Omnibus Press
(A Division of Music Sales Limited)

Cover illustrated & designed by Brian Williamson
Back cover and book designed by Liz Barrand
Text by Jim McCarthy
Book illustrated by Brian Williamson

ISBN: 978.1.84938.701.9
Order No: OP53889

Exclusive Distributors
Music Sales Limited,
14/15 Berners Street,
London, W1T 3LJ.

Music Sales Corporation,
257 Park Avenue South,
New York, NY 10010, USA.

Macmillan Distribution Services,
56 Parkwest Drive
Derrimut, Vic 3030,
Australia.

Printed in Spain.

A catalogue record for this book is available from the British Library.

Visit Omnibus Press on the web at www.omnibuspress.com

MICHAEL JACKSON

INTRODUCTION BY STACEY APPEL

The life of Michael Jackson is a study in contrast. An electrifying entertainer who performed in front of thousands, he was painfully shy when in the company of just a few. His favourite place on Earth was the G-rated Disneyland, but his crotch-grabbing dance moves were considered too raunchy for television. And as a kid star at Motown, he was often described as having an "old soul", but as an adult, his child-like behaviour became tabloid fodder. A very slight, light-footed, soft-spoken man, Michael Jackson was also possessed of such overpowering innovation and creativity that he had no choice but to change the world as he knew it.

Michael was born during the summer 1958 into a Gary, Indiana-dwelling working class family. He showed the first signs of his rhythmic genius while still in diapers when, at a mere one-and-a-half years old, he left mother Katherine speechless as she spotted him dancing, baby bottle in hand, to the whirl of her creaky old washing machine. He would become transfixed while watching idols like James Brown on the TV, and grow irritated when the camera panned up to his face, hindering little Michael from studying the singer's feet. His lightning quick reflexes and superior agility became apparent during those unfortunate moments when papa Joseph tried to discipline his young child – Joe often found himself chasing after Michael who, like Roadrunner escaping Wile E. Coyote, disappeared into thin air, leaving a puff of dust in his wake.

But Michael's gifts were not lost on his father, either. When Joe assembled his musically-inclined offspring into a singing group, it was Michael whom he put front and centre. The Jackson 5 paid their dues by spending their grade school years playing alongside near-naked ladies at local strip bars and competing in talent contests in and around Gary. As the family act became increasingly polished, they graduated to the more legit theatres of the "chitlin' circuit", a series of venues that hosted African American acts. They were invited to audition for Motown where Michael, channeling James Brown in voice, spins, and grunts, so impressed label founder Berry Gordy, Jr. that the record exec made an exception to his rule about never signing another kid act.

By 1970, the entire Jackson clan had high-tailed it to Los Angeles and were enjoying their first taste of chart-topping success with their infectiously funky debut single 'I Want You Back'. Three more consecutive number one songs followed, as did countless television appearances, a cartoon series, Jackson 5-branded merchandise, and millions of delirious young fans. Michael, now almost a teenager, was delighted with the group's ascendancy but also more than a bit wistful; creating music and performing was all he had ever dreamed of, but not being able to join the neighbourhood kids at the playground created a profound sadness within him.

Within a few short years, hit records had all but vanished for the almost grown Jackson 5, leading

Michael and his brothers to quit Motown for greener pastures at CBS. It was there that Michael made *Off The Wall*, the glittery dance floor opera that put him on the map as an adult megastar. Released in '79 just weeks before his 21st birthday, *Off The Wall* boogied in to the public's collective consciousness, in spite of a growing disdain for disco music. The success of the album further set Michael apart from not only his brothers, but from all of the has-been child stars whose careers never recovered from the after-effects of puberty.

When Michael began working on the follow-up album, *Thriller*, he had, of all people, Tchaikovsky on his mind. A classical music fan since he was a child, the singer marveled at the Russian composer's ability to write a piece like *The Nutcracker Suite* in which, in his own words, "every song is a killer." He wondered why a pop record couldn't be crafted in a similar manner, instead of having good songs sandwiched in with album filler. *The Nutcracker* became Michael's blueprint as he set out to create an album which would contain nothing but potential hits.

Thriller was released in November of 1982 and while it was an immediate smash with critics and fans, it was Michael's music videos that helped to elevate it from mere multi-platinum status to the Top-Selling Album of All Time. Of the seven tunes released as singles, only three got the video treatment, but they were unlike anything else that was being aired on the then-fledgling cable channel, MTV. "I would look at what people were doing with video, and I couldn't understand why so much of it seemed so primitive and weak," Michael would later recall in his autobiography. "I wanted something that would glue you to the set, something you'd want to watch over and over." And that's exactly what happened as MTV threw 'Billie Jean' and 'Beat It' into heavy on-air rotation. Even 'Thriller', which clocked in at 14-minutes long, was broadcast once an hour. And no matter how many times we watched them, we remained spellbound. So there we sat, in front of the tube waiting for MJ videos to magically appear, so we could study them closely, memorise the choreography.

Ah yes, the choreography. It was Michael who introduced the large Broadway-style ensemble dance numbers into the music video. His videos also showcased his own dance prowess, which seemed to tamper with everything Isaac Newton ever taught us about the Laws of Motion. Throughout the early part of his career, Michael had proven himself a magnificent mover and shaker, but it was his performance of 'Billie Jean' on the "Motown 25"

concert that became one of the most memorable musical moments in the history of television. While lip-syncing the number-one tune, Michael premiered his version of an old street move called the Backslide. As his legs appeared to be stepping forward, his body coasted backwards, clear across the stage. Punctuated by a quick pop to the tip top of his toes, he renamed the manoeuvre the Moonwalk. The studio audience went bananas, as did the 47 million viewers watching at home. The day after the show was broadcast, Fred Astaire phoned up Michael and declared, "You're a hell of a mover."

The crystal-studded glove he wore during that legendary performance became his signature and we, the fans, honoured our hero by sporting single white mitts that we had embellished ourselves. Replicas of the leather jackets Michael wore in his videos quickly sprung up in clothing boutiques while red, black and white became the most ubiquitous colours in fashion. Michael's face appeared on everything from T-shirts and posters to notebooks and dolls. President Ronald Reagan invited him to the White House,

he won a record-breaking eight Grammy Awards in 1984, penned the charity hit single 'We Are The World', and still had time to star in his own Disney theme park attraction, *Captain EO*. *Thriller* had sold 44 million copies by the time it finally dropped off the charts.

But while Michael seemed as though he could walk on water during the *Thriller* years, the rest of his career would find him struggling to stay afloat as his so-called odd behaviors began to overshadow his artistry. His reclusive nature and reluctance to grant interviews just made the press all the more rabid in their quest for dirt. They raised their eyebrows when he spent time with children, joked about his "relationship" with Bubbles the chimp, and were fascinated by his closeness with Elizabeth Taylor.

What was lost in the murky fog of tabloid journalism, however, was the fact that Michael Jackson albums still sold exceptionally well in spite of the negative press. *Bad* and *Dangerous* both went platinum 30 times over, with *Bad* spawning five number-one songs. Even the double-disc compilation album *HIStory: Past, Present And Future, Book I* sold 20 million units. His short films continued to break artistic ground, from Michael's gravity defying lean in 'Smooth Criminal' to the multi-culti morphing of 'Black Or White' to the retro-futuristic minimalism of 'Scream'. Still, the media focused on his personal business, his marriage to Lisa Marie Presley, and the accusations of child abuse brought against him which led to a circus of a court trial in 2005. After being found not guilty, he all but disappeared from public view for several years, only reemerging to celebrate the 25th anniversary of the album that made him an icon. He began making plans for a series of concerts to be held in London, a wondrous celebration of his lifetime of work. When thousands of tickets sold out within minutes, no one was more surprised than Michael himself. Thanks to the internet, an entirely new generation of kids had discovered his music and videos through websites like YouTube. The likes of Usher, Justin Timberlake, Beyoncé, and Justin Bieber all cited him as a musical influence, and on the fashion runways luxe 1980's style was in the midst of a revival when designers referenced Michael's shoulder pads and gilded military jackets in their collections. And this enlightened clique of youthquakers couldn't have cared less about the gossip reports or the plastic surgery. That was all just so yesterday and, hence, completely irrelevant.

Michael Jackson sadly passed away before the London shows could even begin. As the world tried to come to terms with the death of a beloved, if not quite fully understood idol, a funny thing happened – the dark cloud that had hovered over Michael throughout the latter part of his life finally disappeared. And what was left was his massive body of work, the music and the videos, as well as his creative vision, the hallmarks of which will forever be imprinted into the work of so many artists today and in years to come.

If it is true that Michael Jackson never really grew up then Neverland celebrates Michael's life in a way that he would probably have appreciated – as a graphic book. In many ways his life was a cartoon fantasy – and his story is brought to life within these pages by Brian Williamson's vivid artwork and Jim McCarthy's dramatic script.

Stacey Appel is the author of Michael Jackson Style due for publication by Omnibus Press in 2012.

PROLOGUE

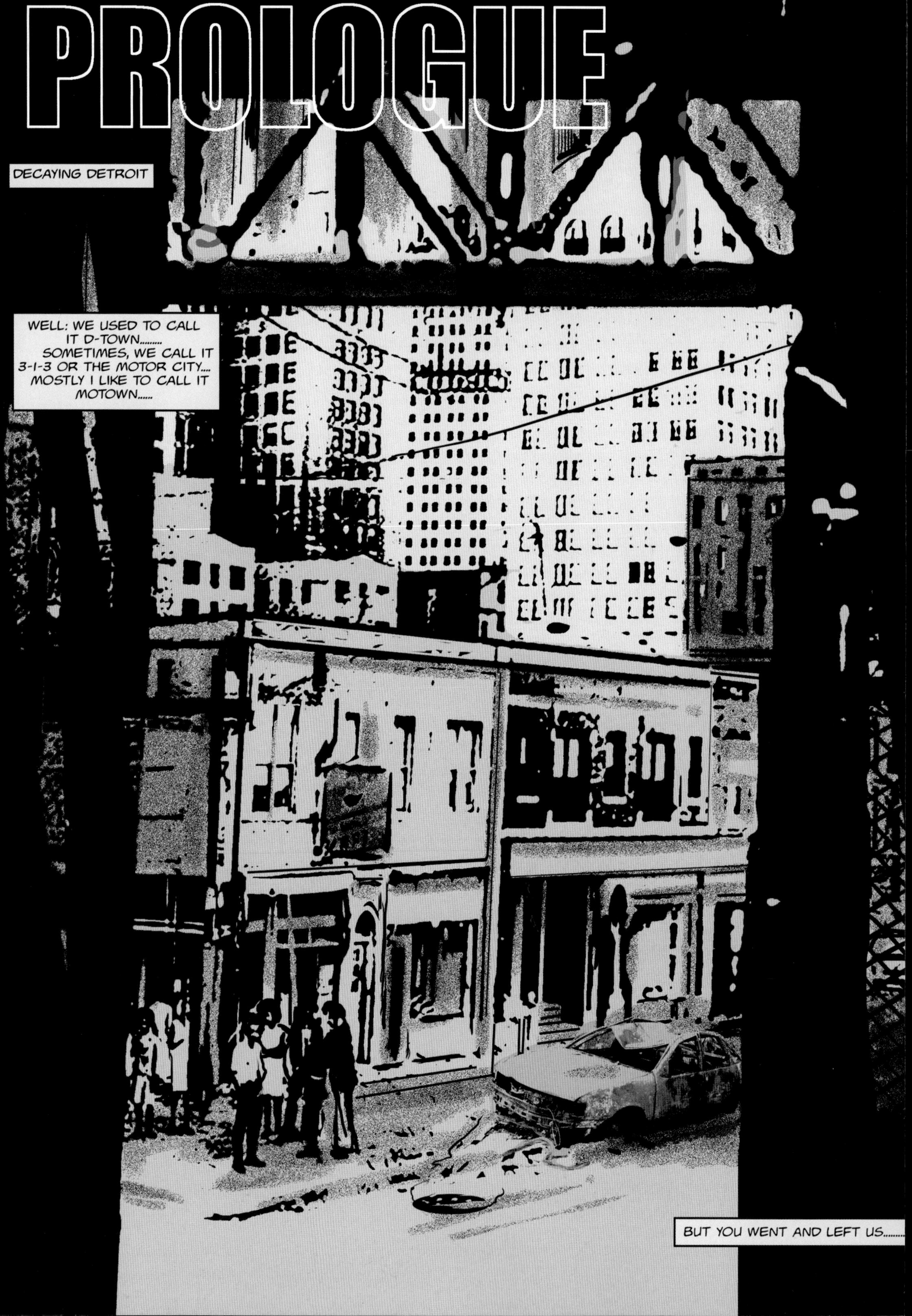
DECAYING DETROIT
WELL: WE USED TO CALL IT D-TOWN......... SOMETIMES, WE CALL IT 3-1-3 OR THE MOTOR CITY.... MOSTLY I LIKE TO CALL IT MOTOWN......
BUT YOU WENT AND LEFT US.........

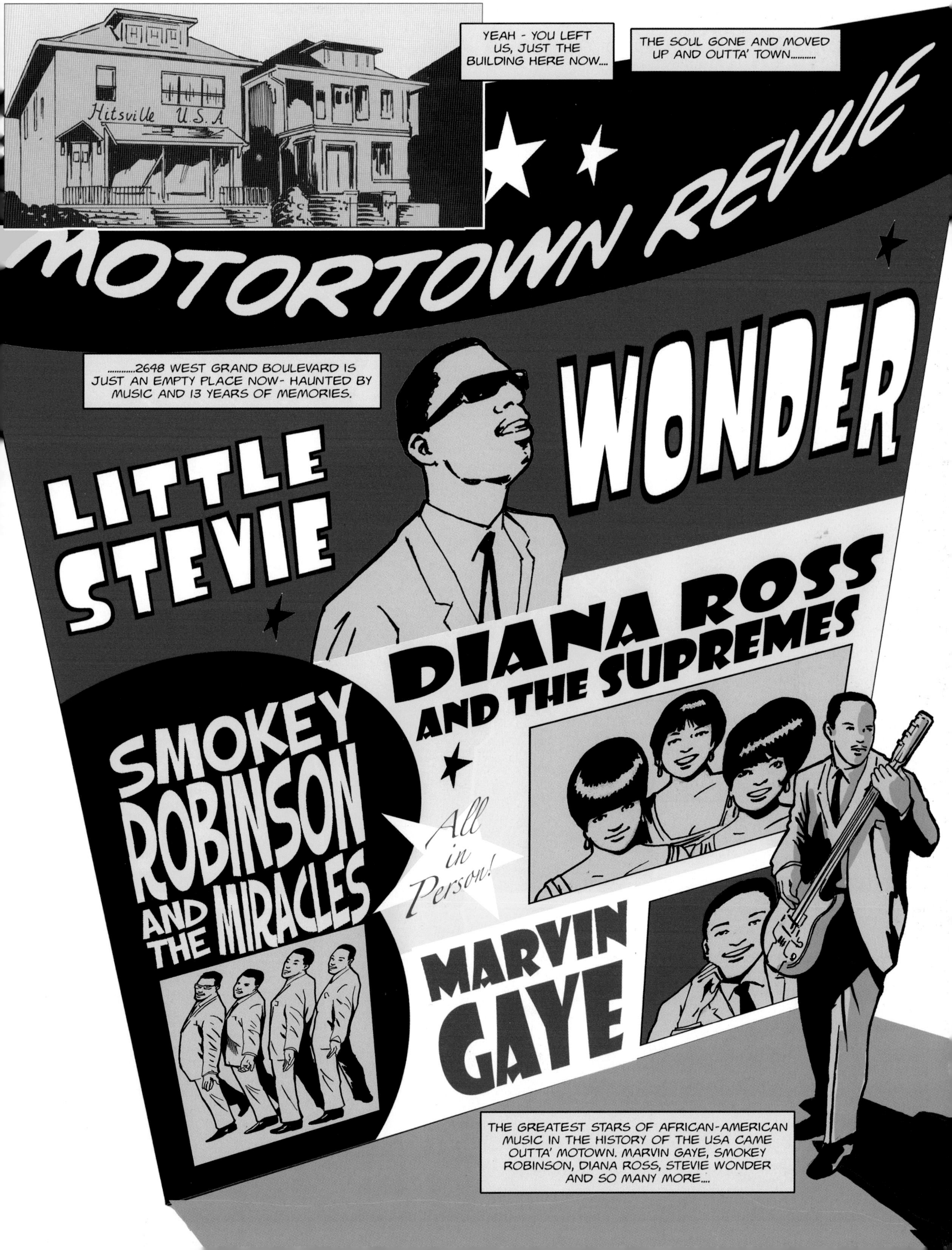
Hitsville U.S.A
YEAH - YOU LEFT US, JUST THE BUILDING HERE NOW....
THE SOUL GONE AND MOVED UP AND OUTTA' TOWN..........
MOTORTOWN REVUE
..........2648 WEST GRAND BOULEVARD IS JUST AN EMPTY PLACE NOW- HAUNTED BY MUSIC AND 13 YEARS OF MEMORIES.
LITTLE STEVIE WONDER
DIANA ROSS AND THE SUPREMES
SMOKEY ROBINSON AND THE MIRACLES
All in Person!
MARVIN GAYE
THE GREATEST STARS OF AFRICAN-AMERICAN MUSIC IN THE HISTORY OF THE USA CAME OUTTA' MOTOWN. MARVIN GAYE, SMOKEY ROBINSON, DIANA ROSS, STEVIE WONDER AND SO MANY MORE....

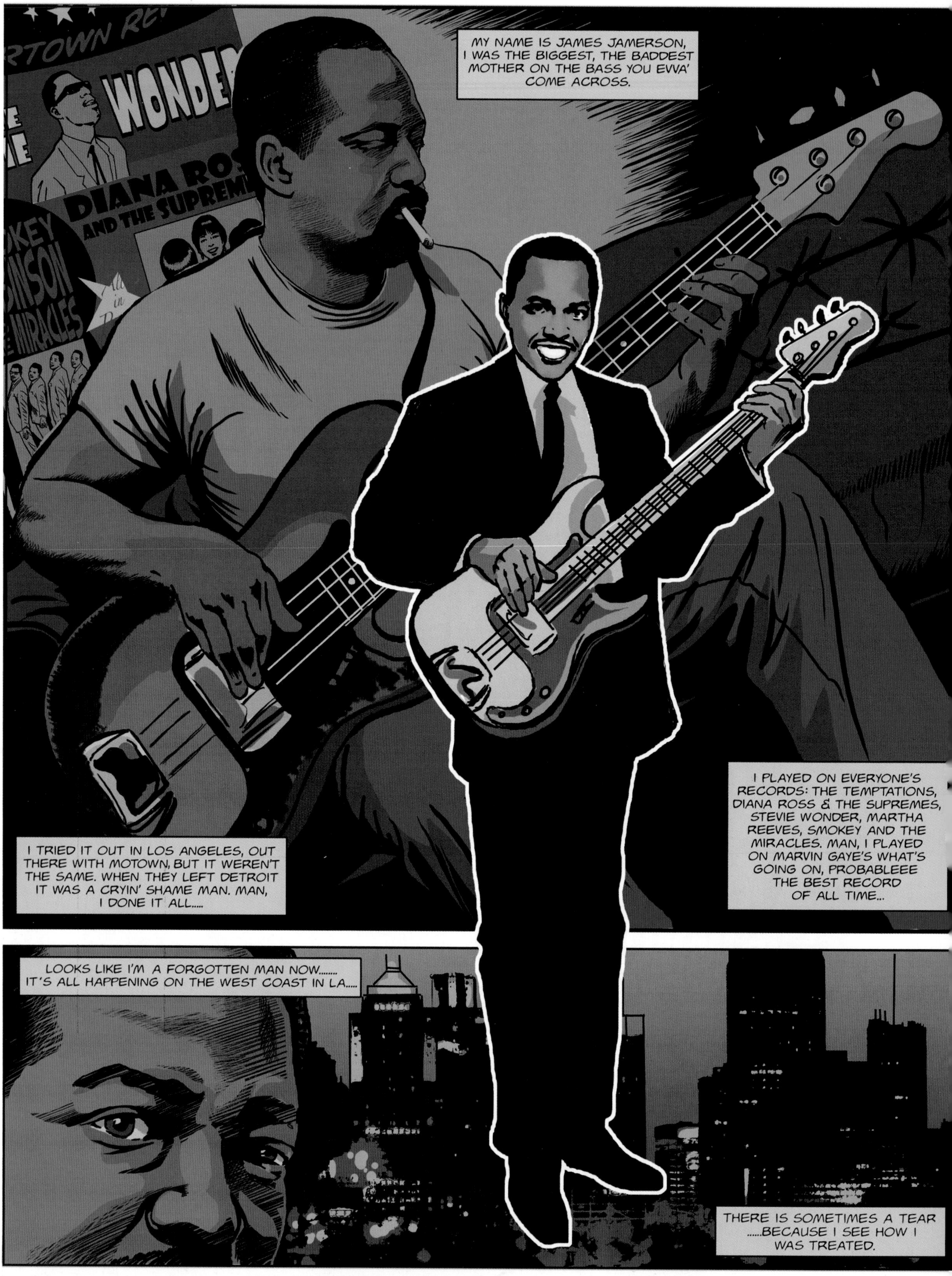
MY NAME IS JAMES JAMERSON, I WAS THE BIGGEST, THE BADDEST MOTHER ON THE BASS YOU EVVA' COME ACROSS.
I PLAYED ON EVERYONE'S RECORDS: THE TEMPTATIONS, DIANA ROSS & THE SUPREMES, STEVIE WONDER, MARTHA REEVES, SMOKEY AND THE MIRACLES. MAN, I PLAYED ON MARVIN GAYE'S WHAT'S GOING ON, PROBABLEEE THE BEST RECORD OF ALL TIME...
I TRIED IT OUT IN LOS ANGELES, OUT THERE WITH MOTOWN, BUT IT WEREN'T THE SAME. WHEN THEY LEFT DETROIT IT WAS A CRYIN' SHAME MAN. MAN, I DONE IT ALL.....
LOOKS LIKE I'M A FORGOTTEN MAN NOW........ IT'S ALL HAPPENING ON THE WEST COAST IN LA.....
THERE IS SOMETIMES A TEAR ......BECAUSE I SEE HOW I WAS TREATED.

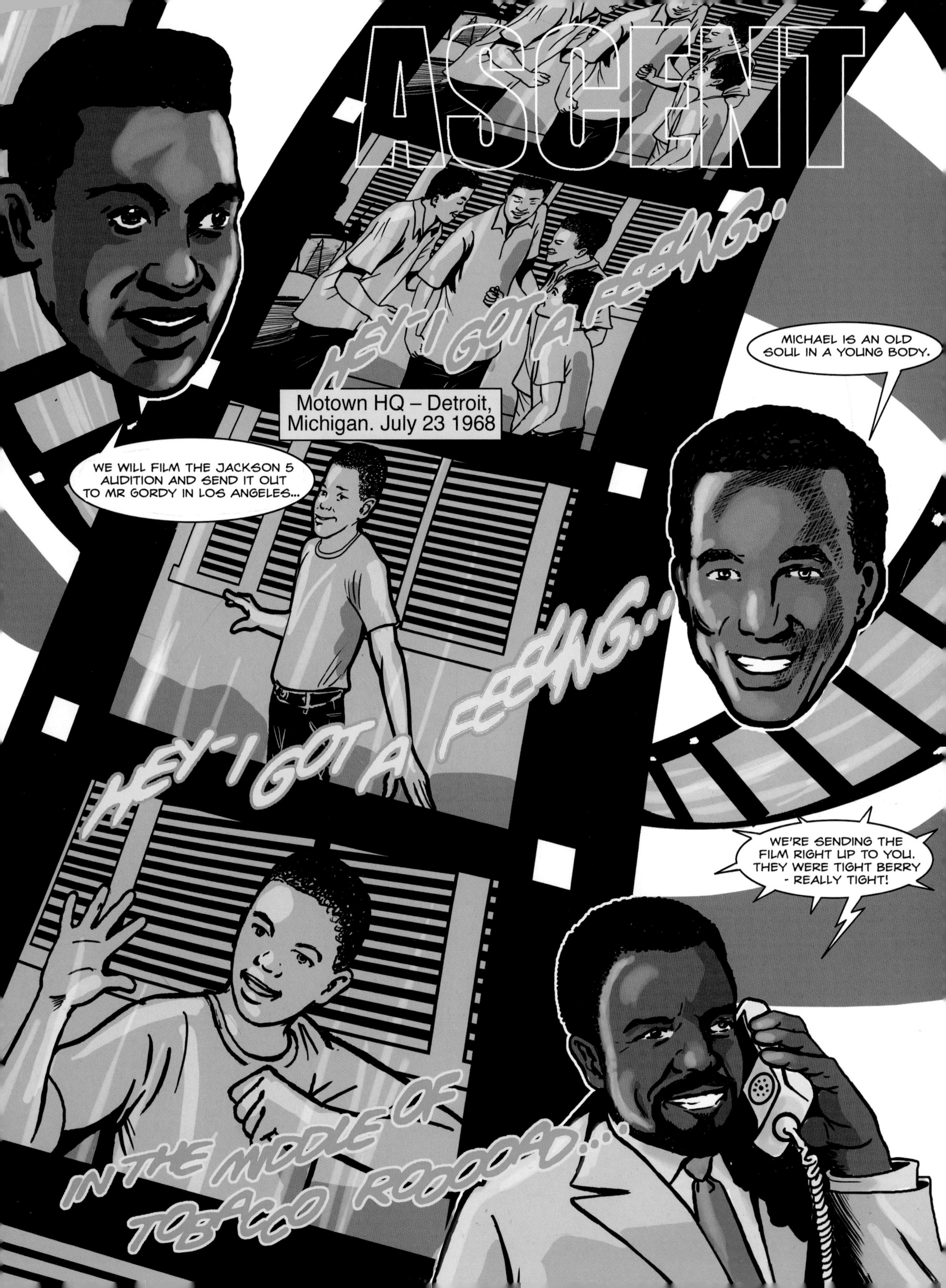
ASCENT
HEY-I GOT A FEELING...
Motown HQ – Detroit, Michigan. July 23 1968
WE WILL FILM THE JACKSON 5 AUDITION AND SEND IT OUT TO MR GORDY IN LOS ANGELES...
MICHAEL IS AN OLD SOUL IN A YOUNG BODY.
HEY-I GOT A FEELING...
WE'RE SENDING THE FILM RIGHT UP TO YOU. THEY WERE TIGHT BERRY - REALLY TIGHT!
IN THE MIDDLE OF TOBACCO ROOOOAD...

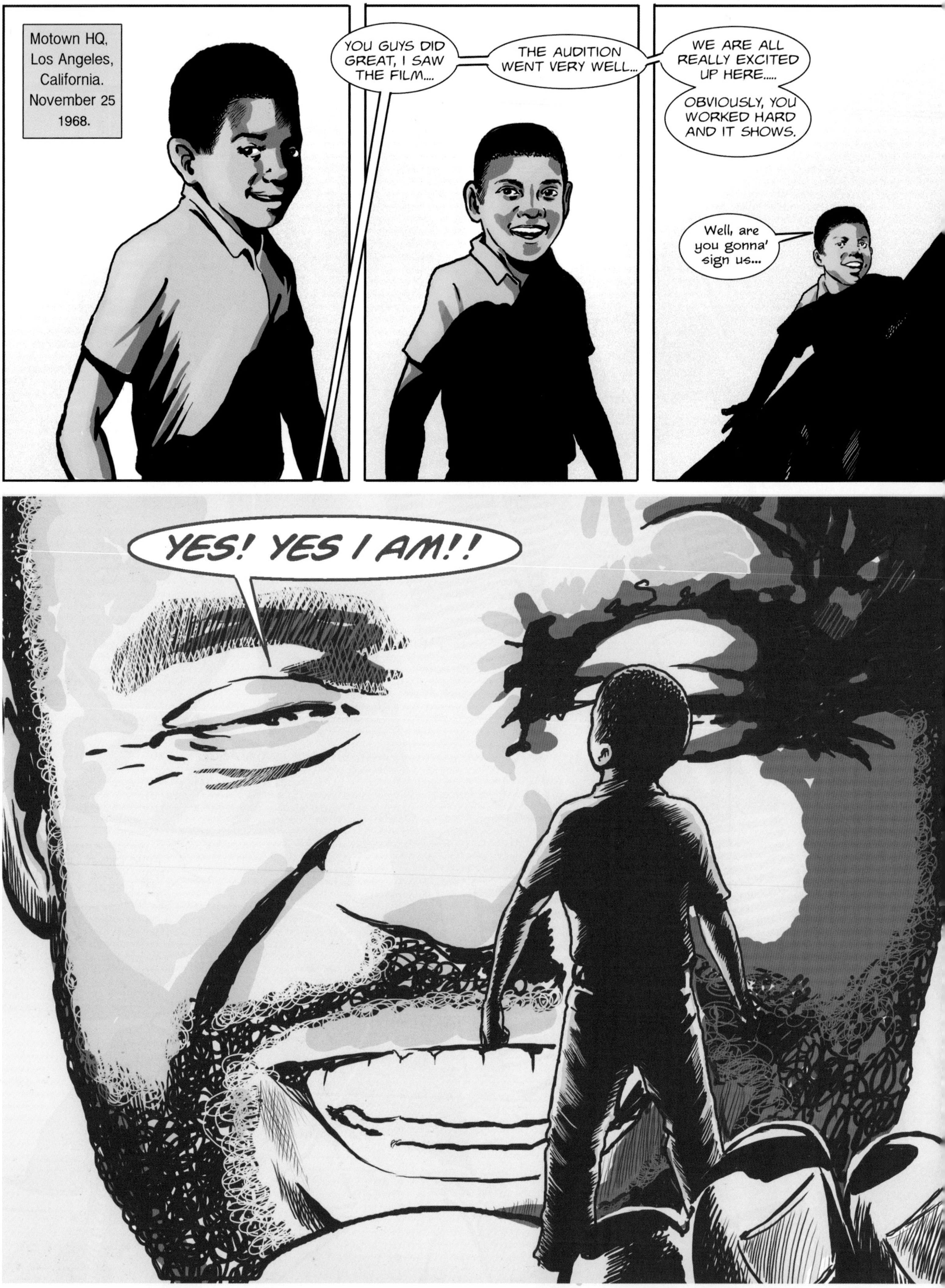
Motown HQ, Los Angeles, California. November 25 1968.
YOU GUYS DID GREAT, I SAW THE FILM....
THE AUDITION WENT VERY WELL...
WE ARE ALL REALLY EXCITED UP HERE.....
OBVIOUSLY, YOU WORKED HARD AND IT SHOWS.
Well, are you gonna' sign us...
YES! YES I AM!!

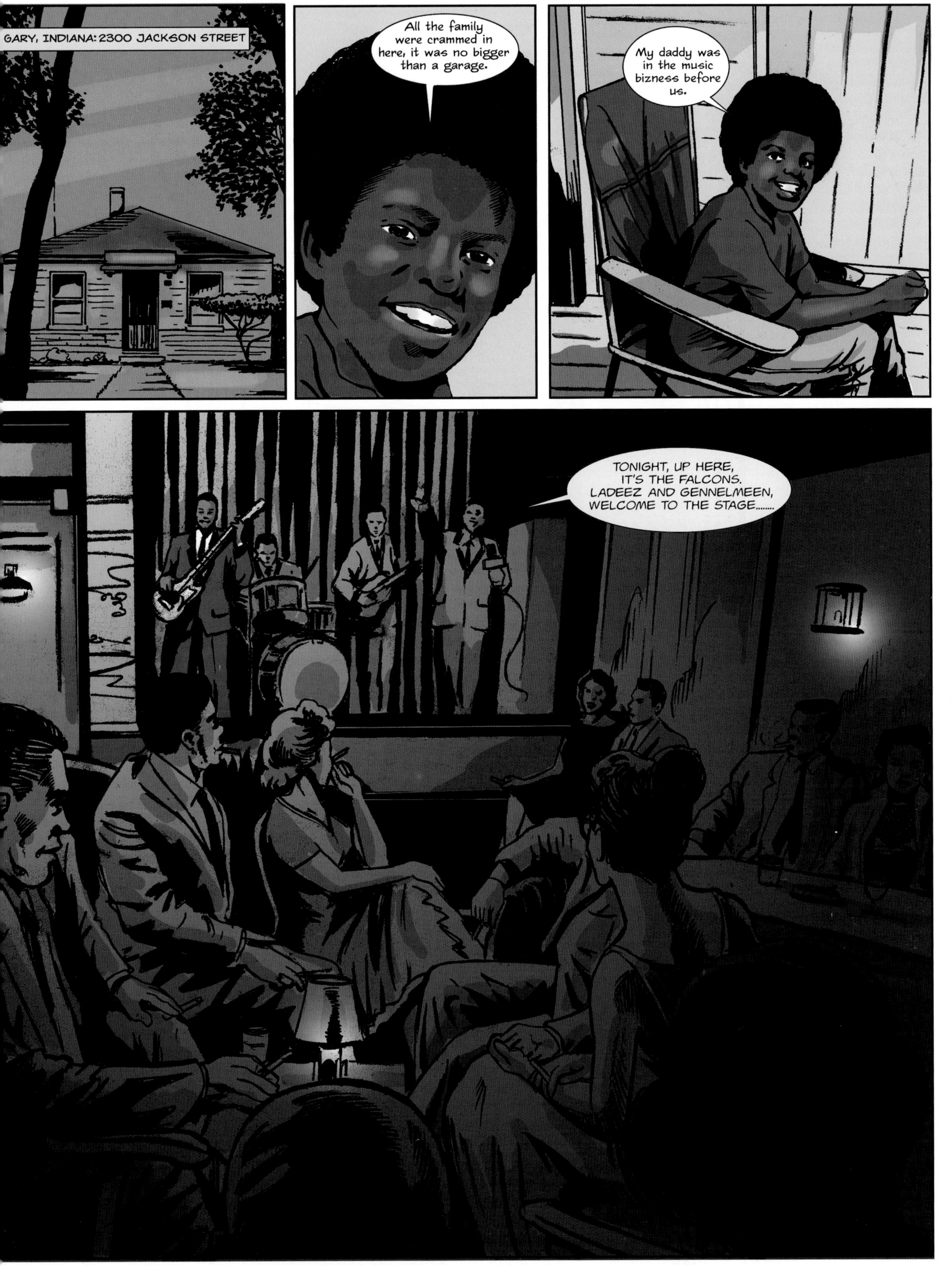
GARY, INDIANA: 2300 JACKSON STREET
All the family were crammed in here, it was no bigger than a garage.
My daddy was in the music bizness before us.
TONIGHT, UP HERE, IT'S THE FALCONS. LADEEZ AND GENNELMEEN, WELCOME TO THE STAGE........

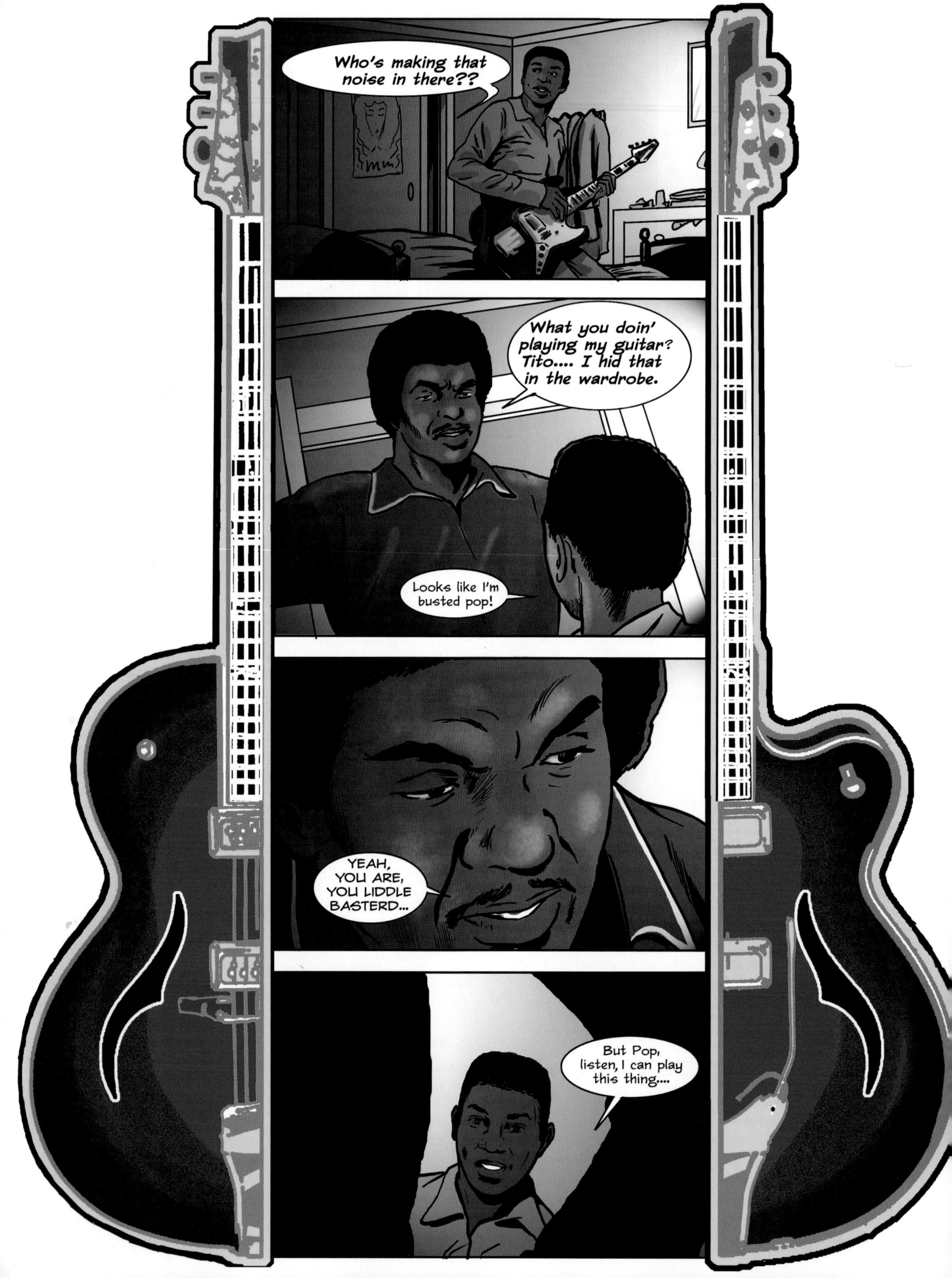
Who's making that noise in there??
What you doin' playing my guitar? Tito.... I hid that in the wardrobe.
Looks like I'm busted pop!
YEAH, YOU ARE, YOU LIDDLE BASTERD...
But Pop, listen, I can play this thing....

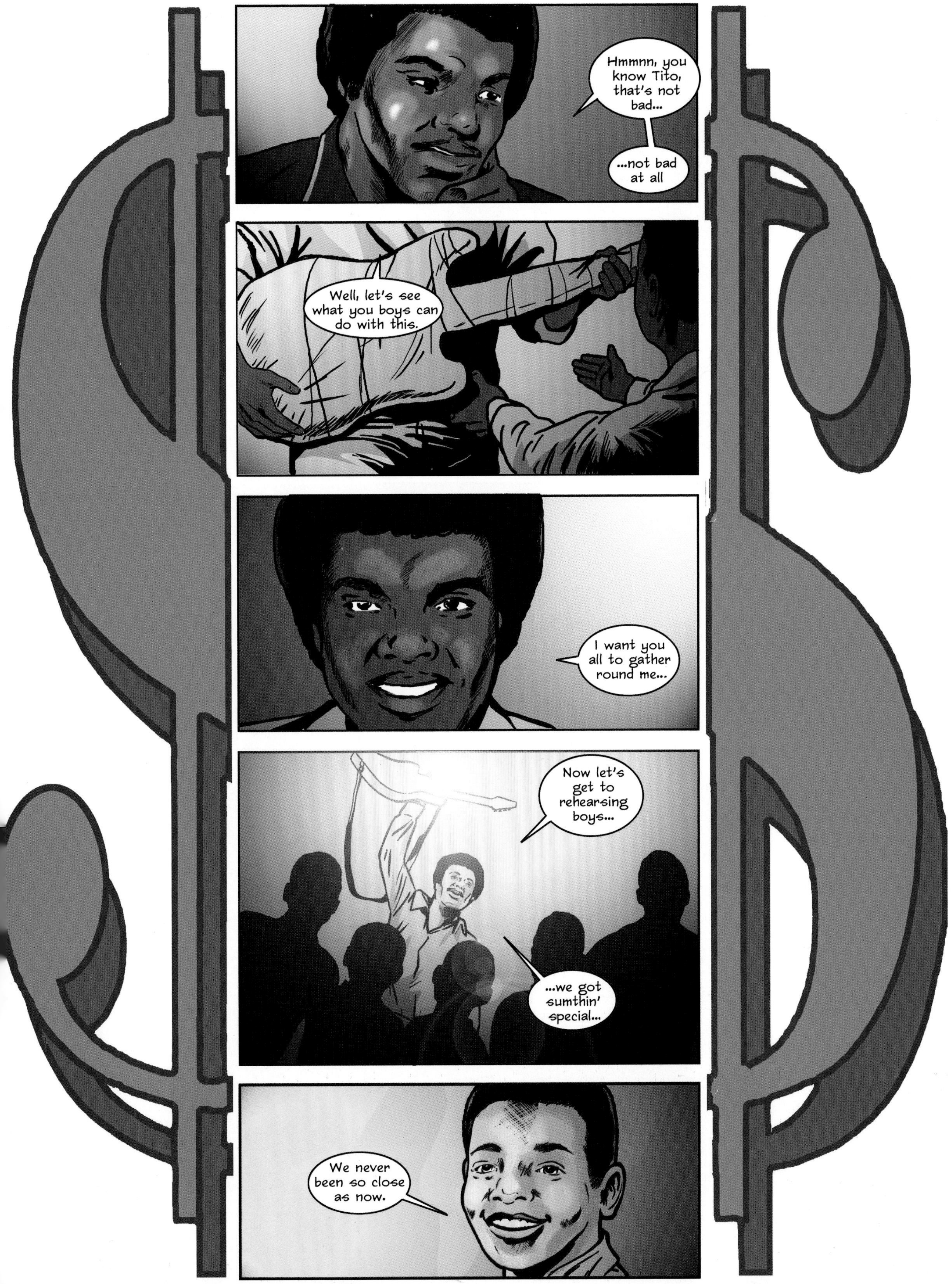

Hmmnn, you know Tito, that's not bad...
...not bad at all
Well, let's see what you boys can do with this.
I want you all to gather round me...
Now let's get to rehearsing boys...
...we got sumthin' special...
We never been so close as now.

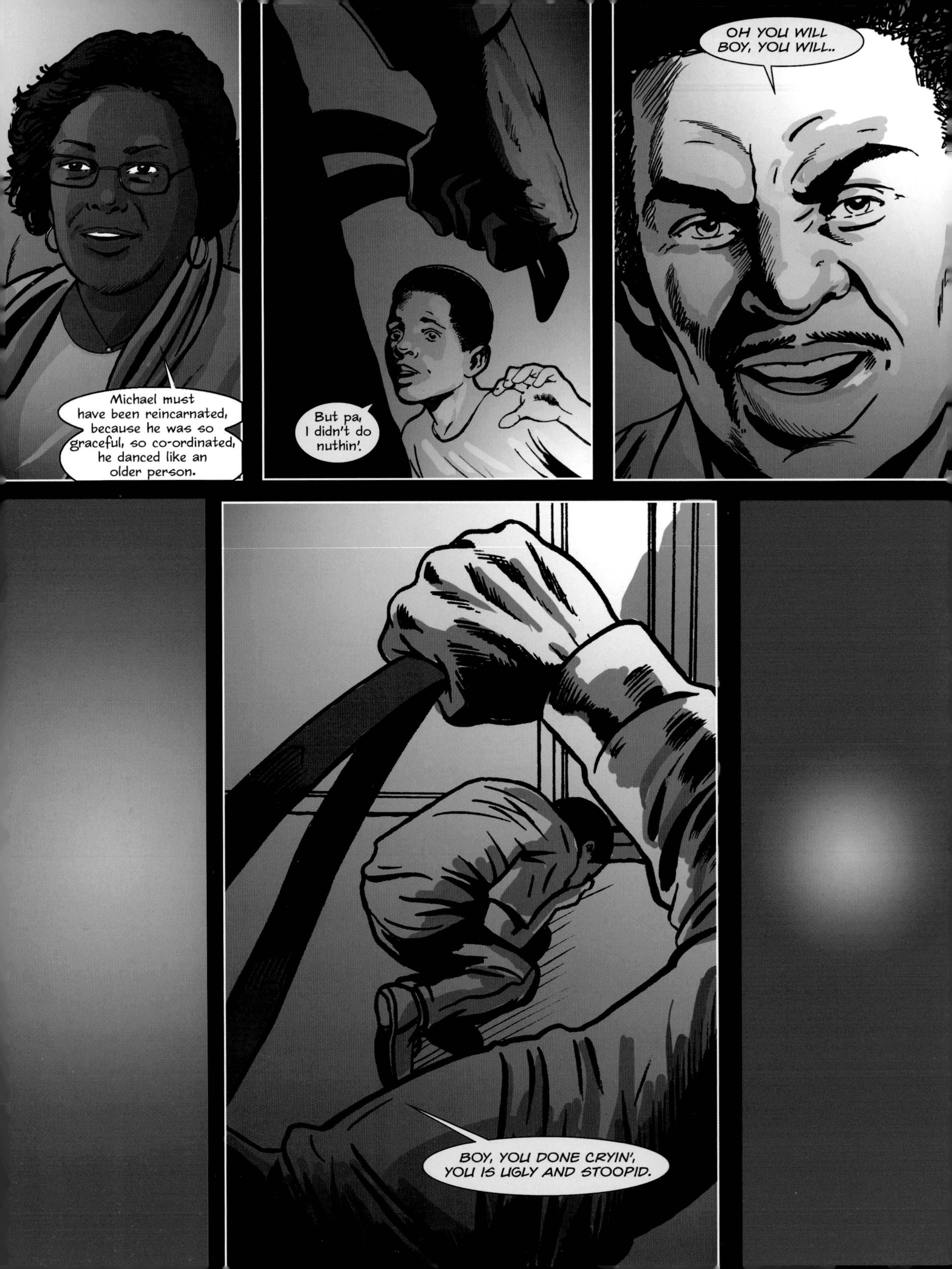
Michael must have been reincarnated, because he was so graceful, so co-ordinated, he danced like an older person.
But pa, I didn't do nuthin'.
OH YOU WILL BOY, YOU WILL..
BOY, YOU DONE CRYIN', YOU IS UGLY AND STOOPID.

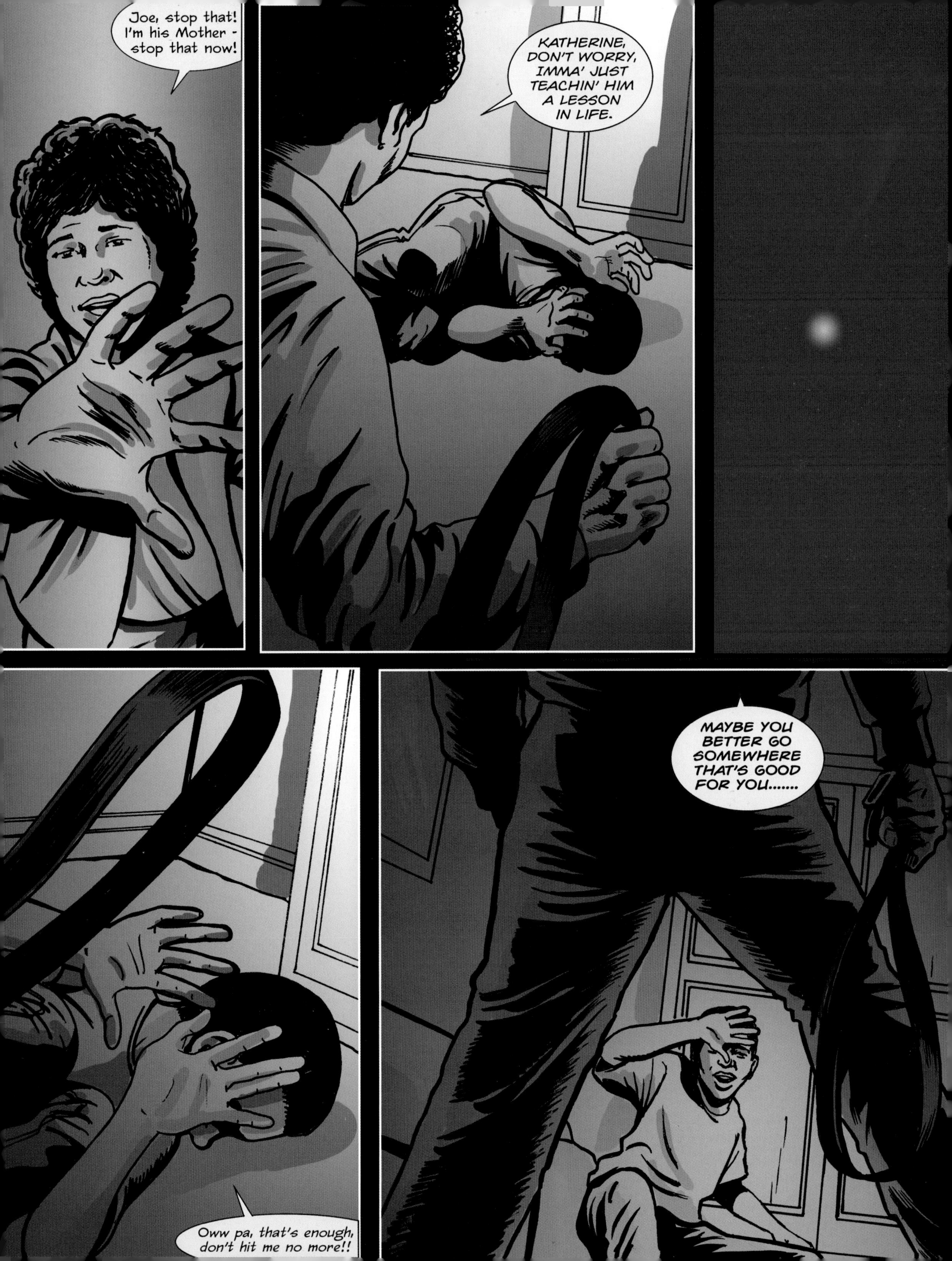
Joe, stop that! I'm his Mother - stop that now!
KATHERINE, DON'T WORRY, IMMA' JUST TEACHIN' HIM A LESSON IN LIFE.
Oww pa, that's enough, don't hit me no more!!
MAYBE YOU BETTER GO SOMEWHERE THAT'S GOOD FOR YOU.......

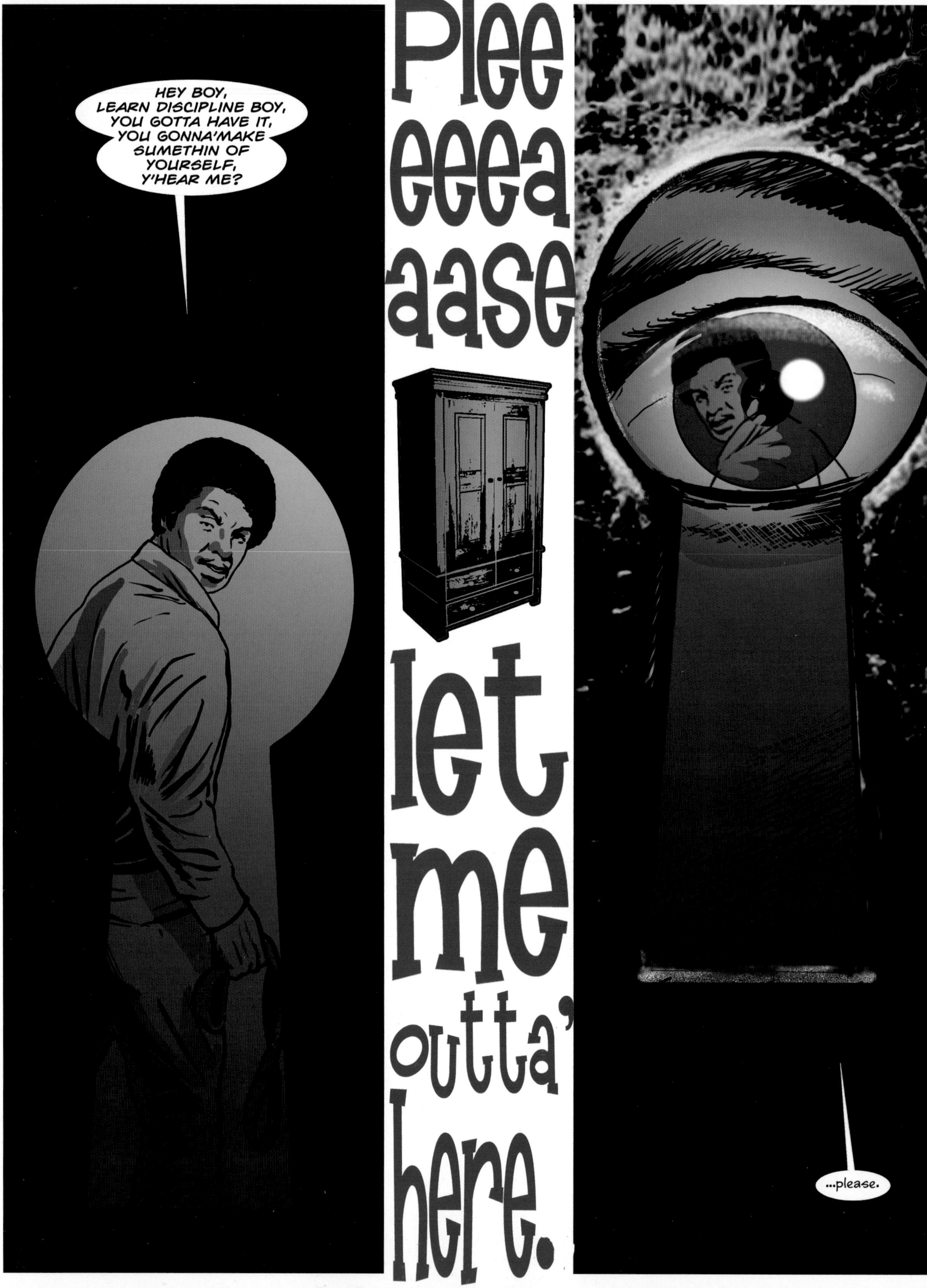
HEY BOY, LEARN DISCIPLINE BOY, YOU GOTTA HAVE IT, YOU GONNA'MAKE SUMETHIN OF YOURSELF, Y'HEAR ME?
Plee eeea aase
let me outta' here.
...please.

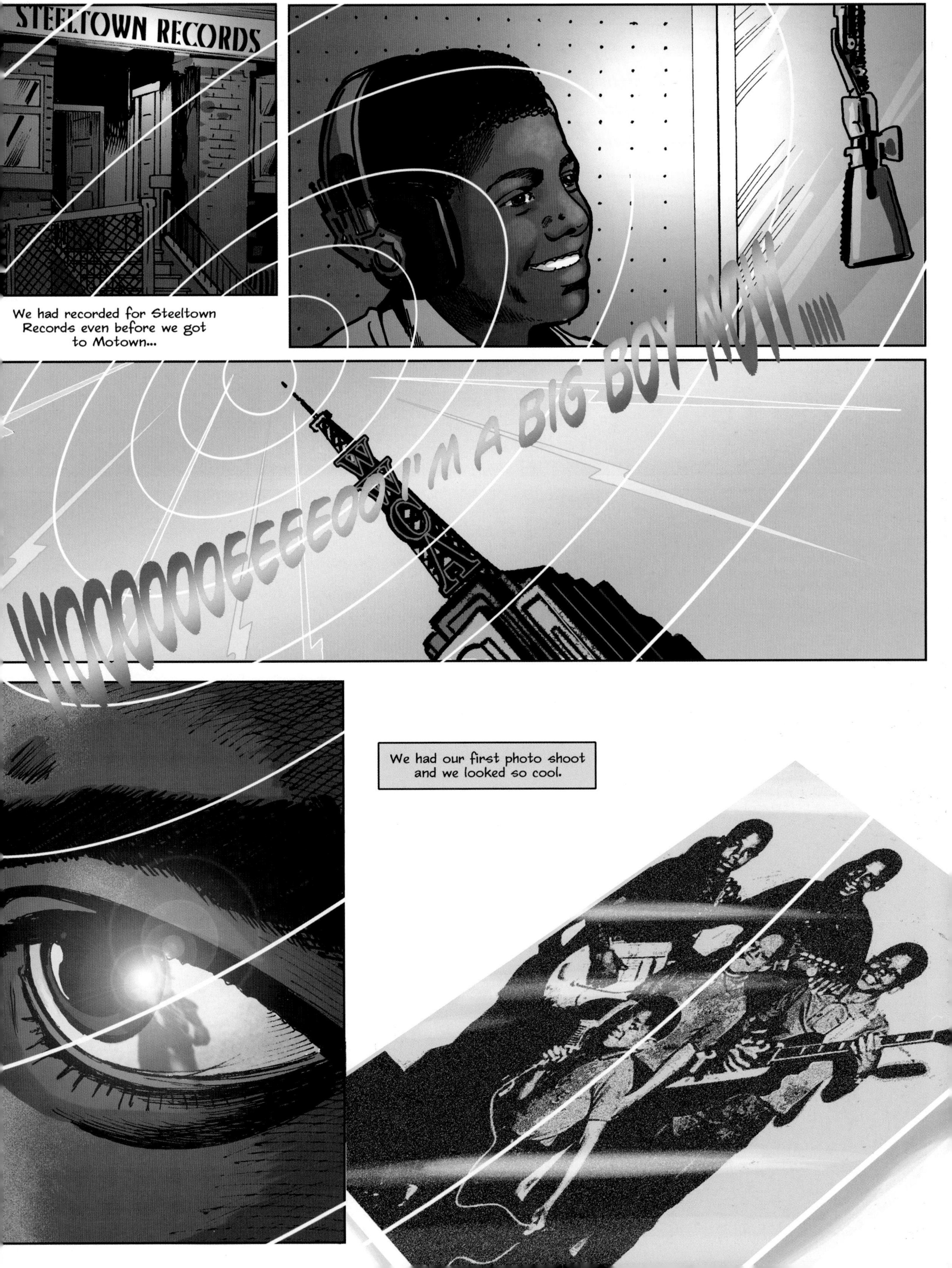
STEELTOWN RECORDS
We had recorded for Steeltown Records even before we got to Motown...
WOOOOOOEEEEEOO I'M A BIG BOY NOW!!!!!!
WVCA
We had our first photo shoot and we looked so cool.

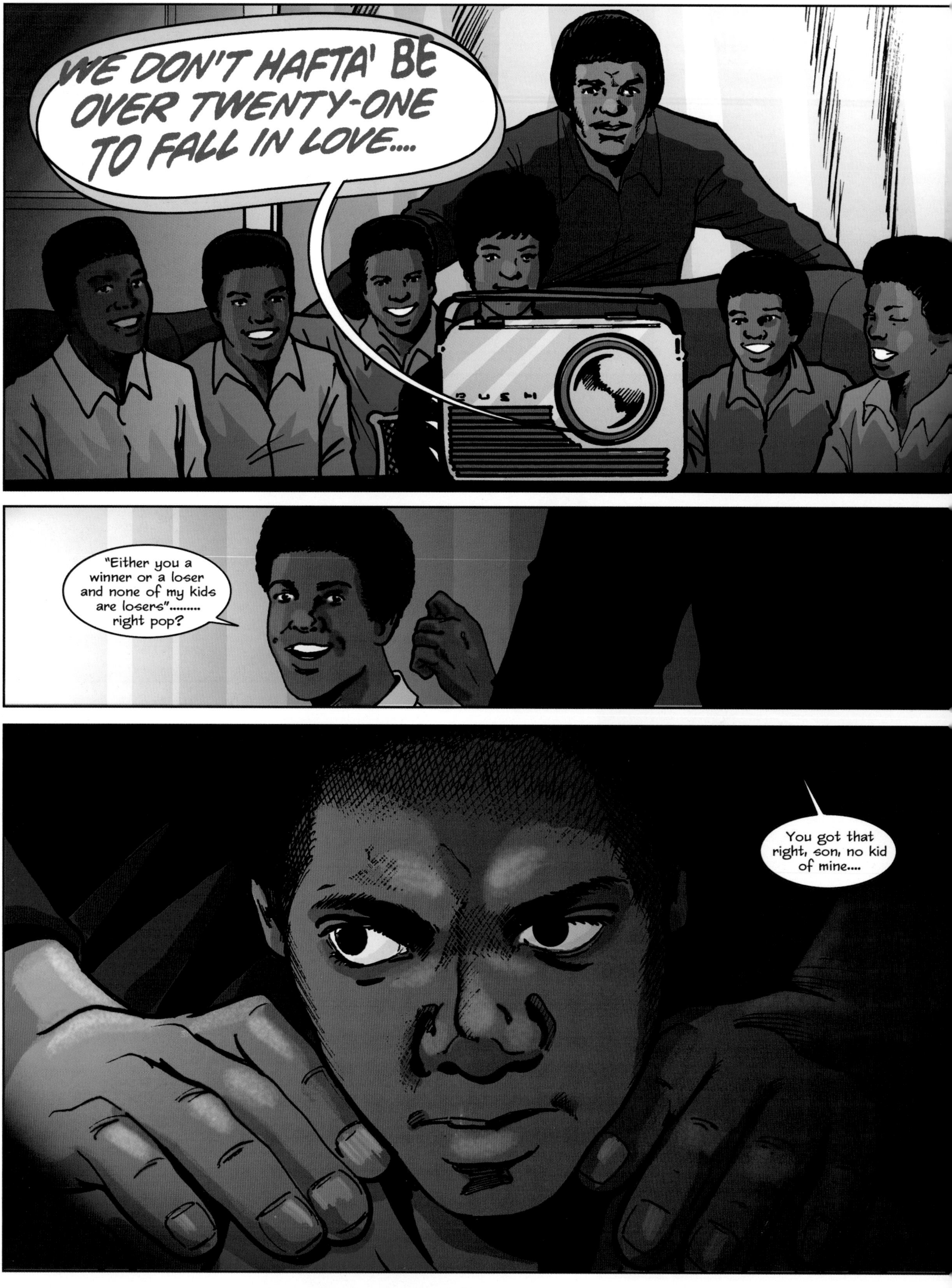
WE DON'T HAFTA' BE OVER TWENTY-ONE TO FALL IN LOVE....
RUSH
"Either you a winner or a loser and none of my kids are losers"......... right pop?
You got that right, son, no kid of mine....

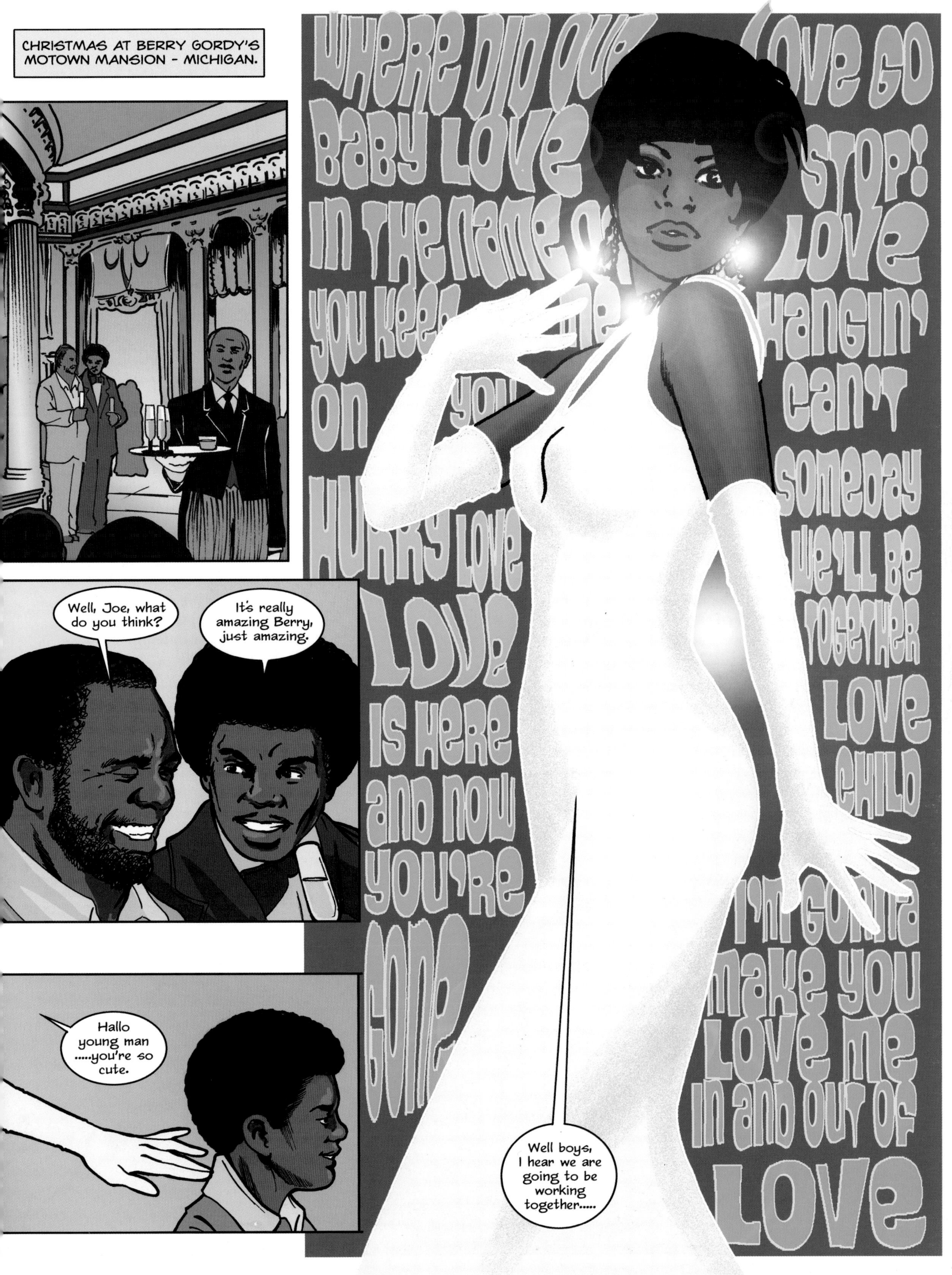
CHRISTMAS AT BERRY GORDY'S MOTOWN MANSION - MICHIGAN.
Well, Joe, what do you think?
It's really amazing Berry, just amazing.
Hallo young man .....you're so cute.
Well boys, I hear we are going to be working together.....

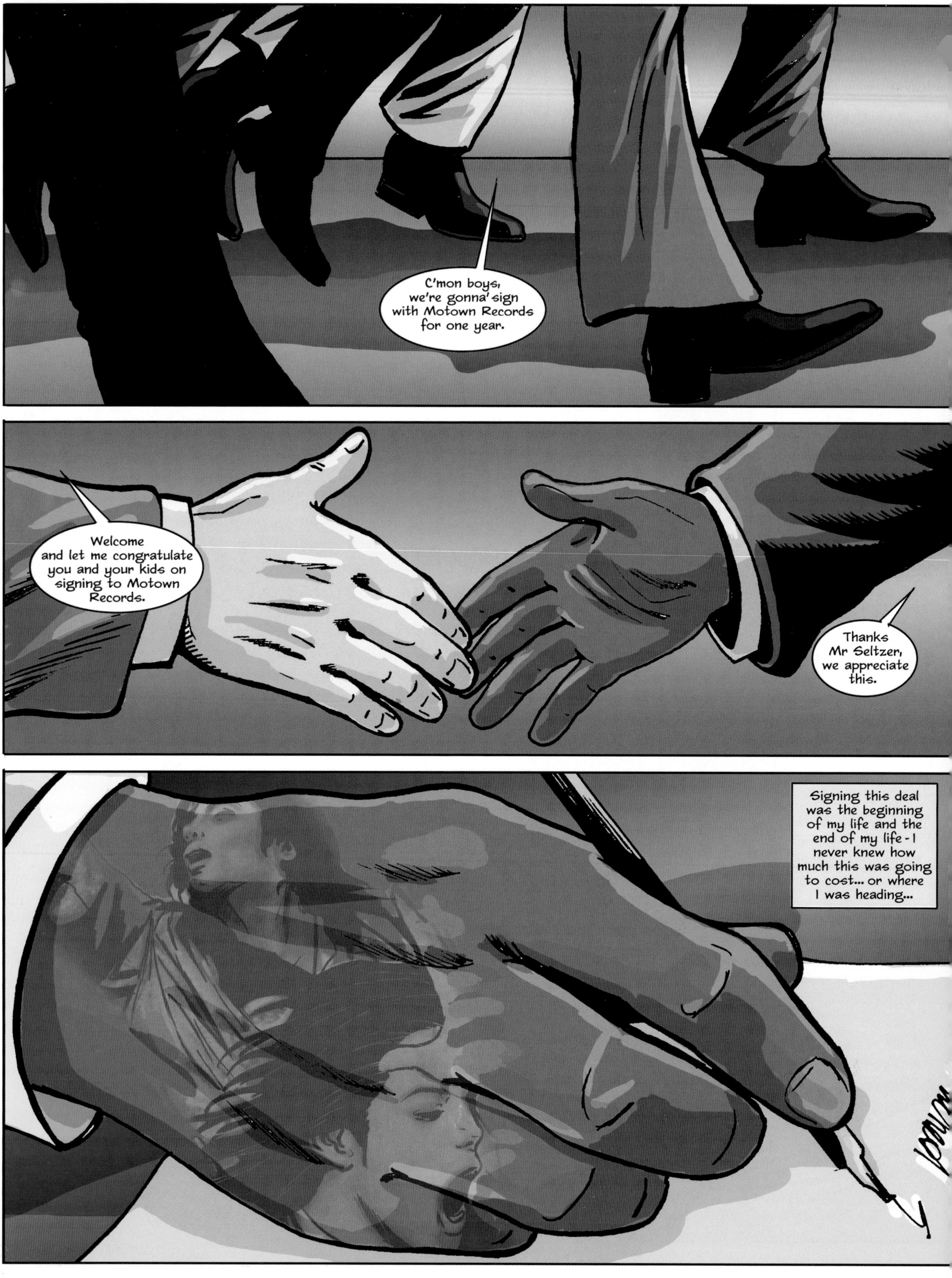
C'mon boys, we're gonna' sign with Motown Records for one year.
Welcome and let me congratulate you and your kids on signing to Motown Records.
Thanks Mr Seltzer, we appreciate this.
Signing this deal was the beginning of my life and the end of my life - I never knew how much this was going to cost... or where I was heading...

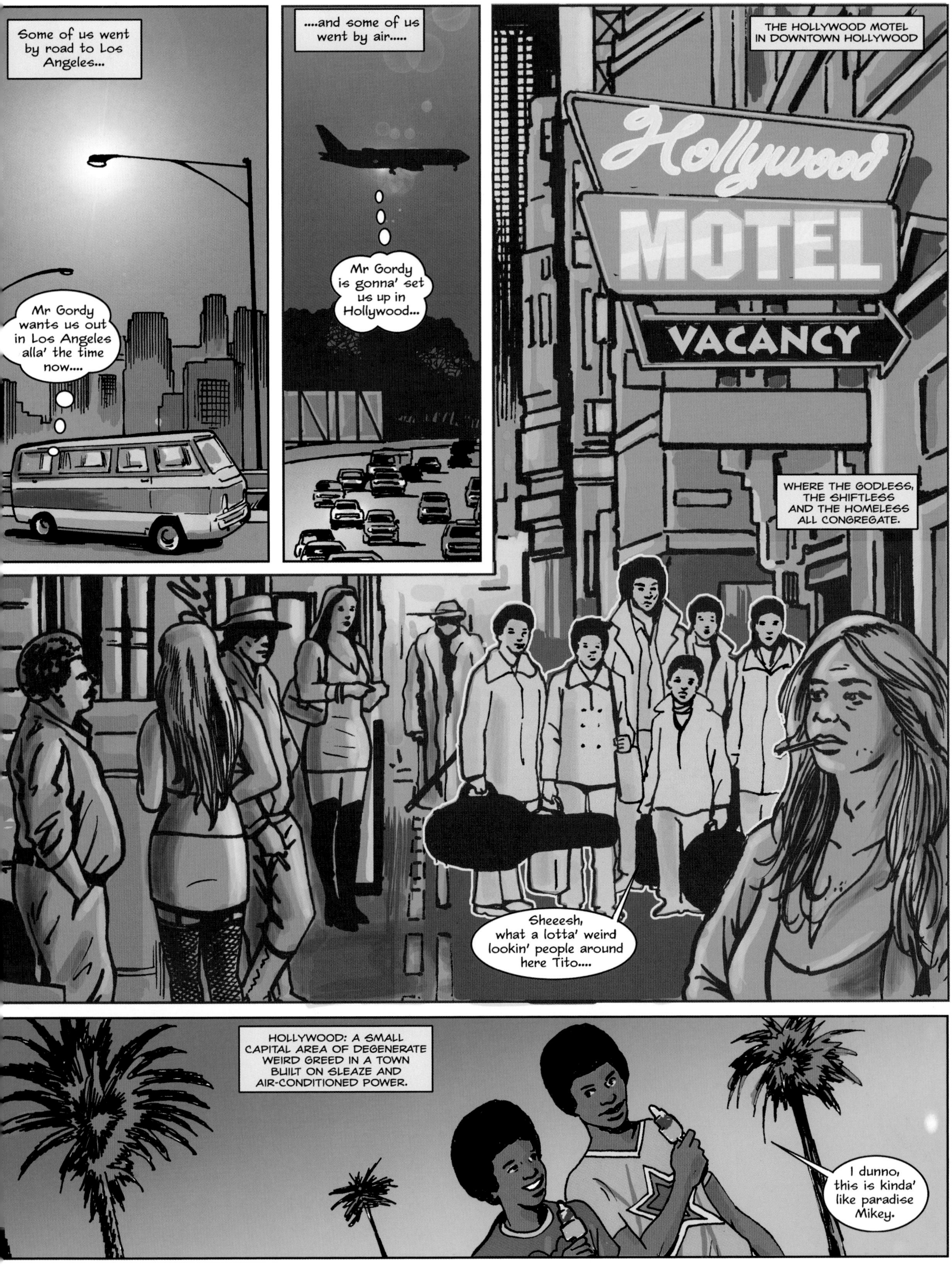
Some of us went by road to Los Angeles...
Mr Gordy wants us out in Los Angeles alla' the time now....
....and some of us went by air.....
Mr Gordy is gonna' set us up in Hollywood...
THE HOLLYWOOD MOTEL IN DOWNTOWN HOLLYWOOD
Hollywood
MOTEL
VACANCY
WHERE THE GODLESS, THE SHIFTLESS AND THE HOMELESS ALL CONGREGATE.
Sheeesh, what a lotta' weird lookin' people around here Tito....
HOLLYWOOD: A SMALL CAPITAL AREA OF DEGENERATE WEIRD GREED IN A TOWN BUILT ON SLEAZE AND AIR-CONDITIONED POWER.
I dunno, this is kinda' like paradise Mikey.

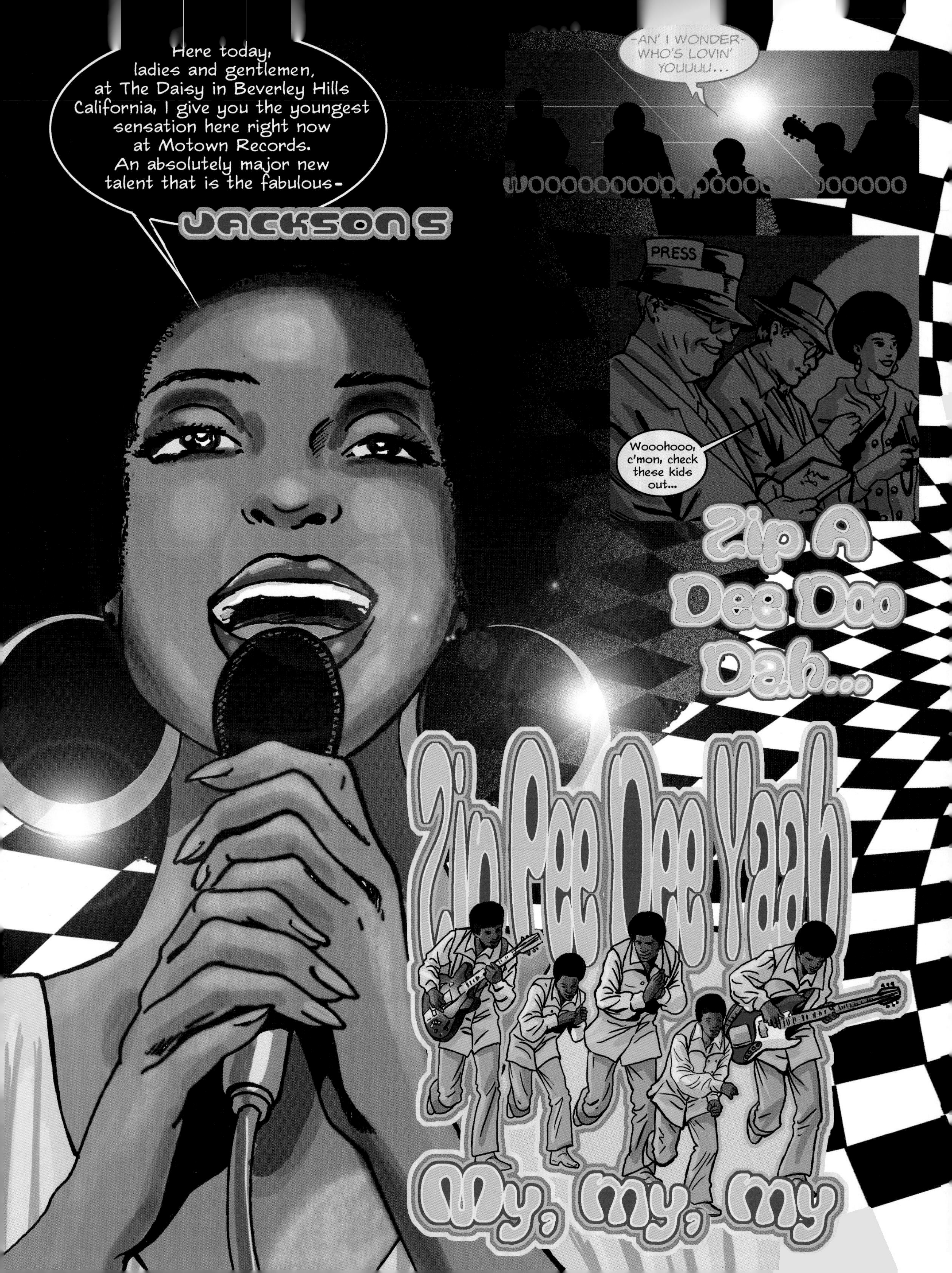
Here today, ladies and gentlemen, at The Daisy in Beverley Hills California, I give you the youngest sensation here right now at Motown Records. An absolutely major new talent that is the fabulous-
JACKSON 5
-AN' I WONDER-
WHO'S LOVIN'
YOUUUU...
PRESS
Wooohooo, c'mon, check these kids out...
Zip A
Dee Doo
Dah...
Zip Pee Dee Yaah
My, my, my

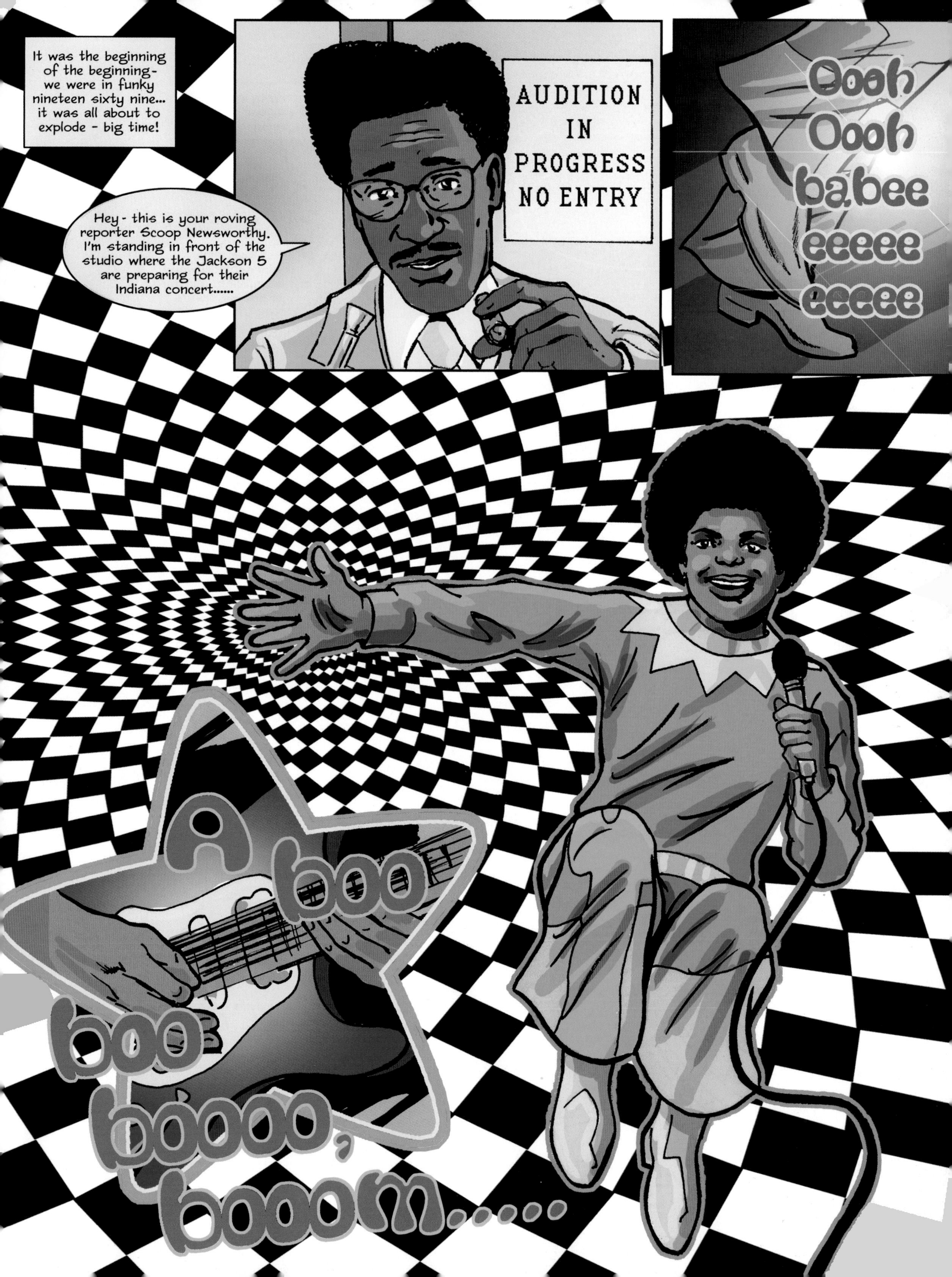

It was the beginning of the beginning- we were in funky nineteen sixty nine... it was all about to explode - big time!
AUDITION IN PROGRESS NO ENTRY
Hey - this is your roving reporter Scoop Newsworthy. I'm standing in front of the studio where the Jackson 5 are preparing for their Indiana concert......
Oooh Oooh babee eeeee eeeee
A boo boo boo booooo, booom.....

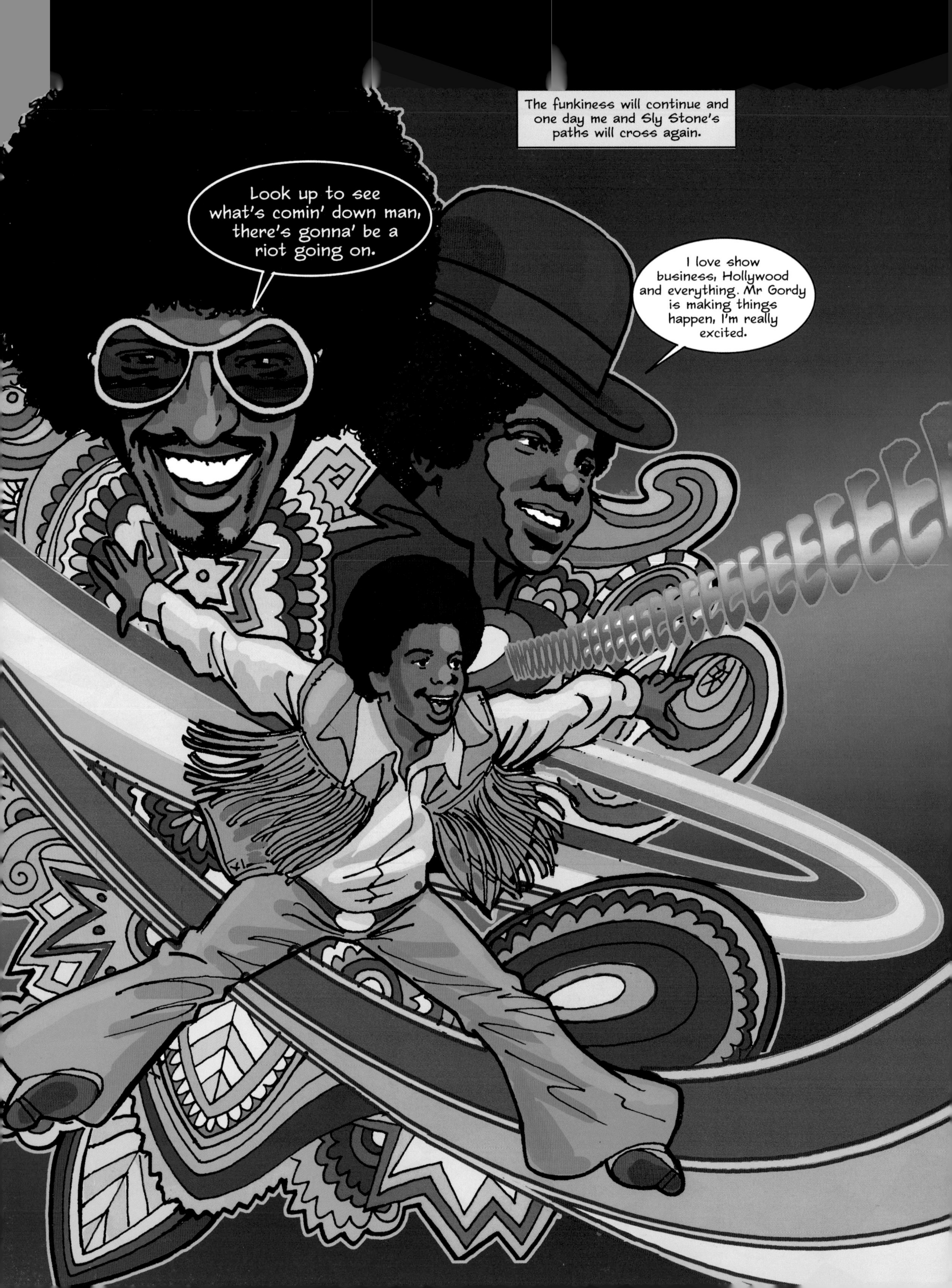
The funkiness will continue and one day me and Sly Stone's paths will cross again.
Look up to see what's comin' down man, there's gonna' be a riot going on.
I love show business, Hollywood and everything. Mr Gordy is making things happen, I'm really excited.
WHOOOOOOEEEEEEEEEEEEEEEEEEE

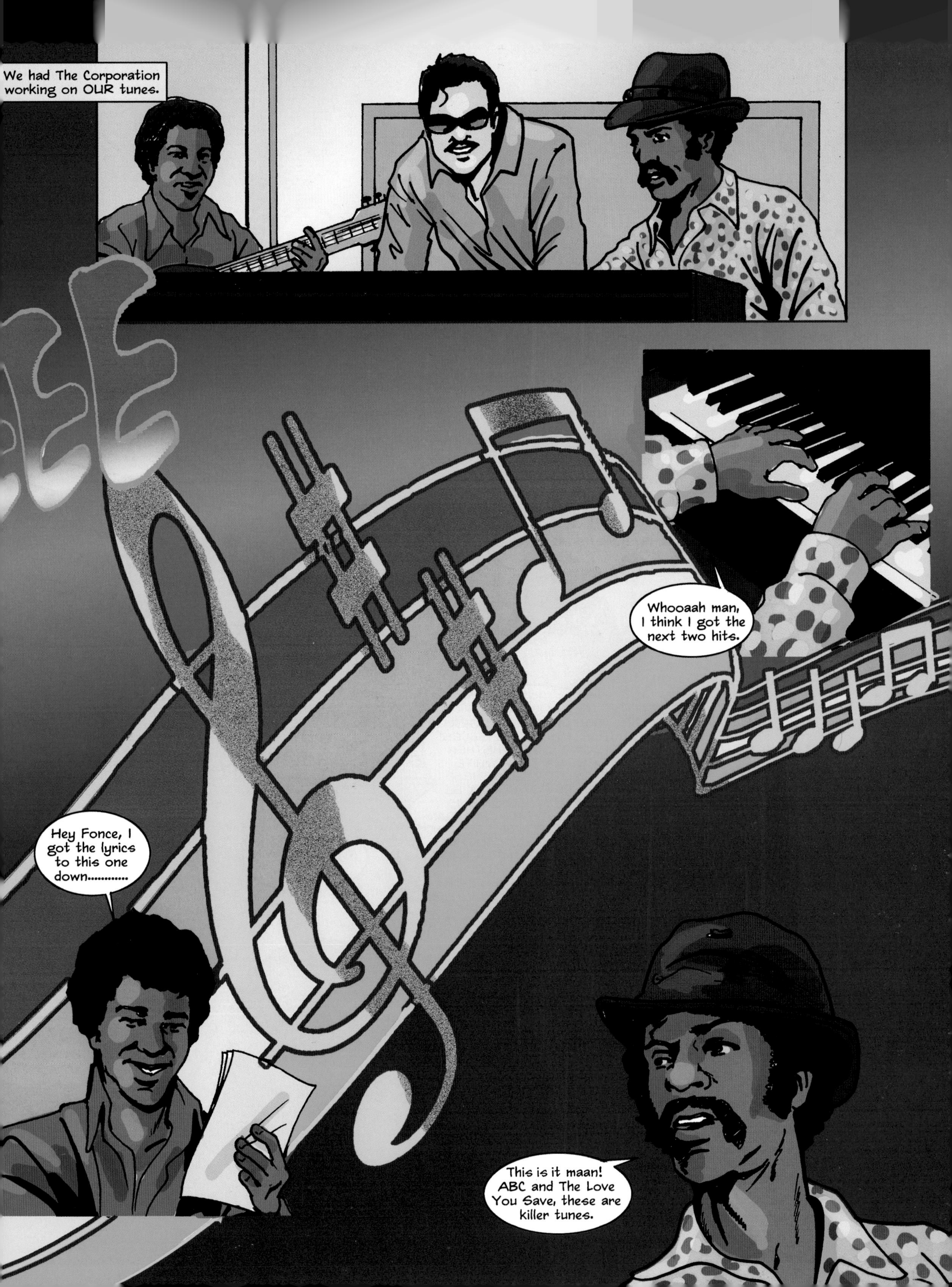
We had The Corporation working on OUR tunes.
Whooaah man, I think I got the next two hits.
Hey Fonce, I got the lyrics to this one down............
This is it maan! ABC and The Love You Save, these are killer tunes.

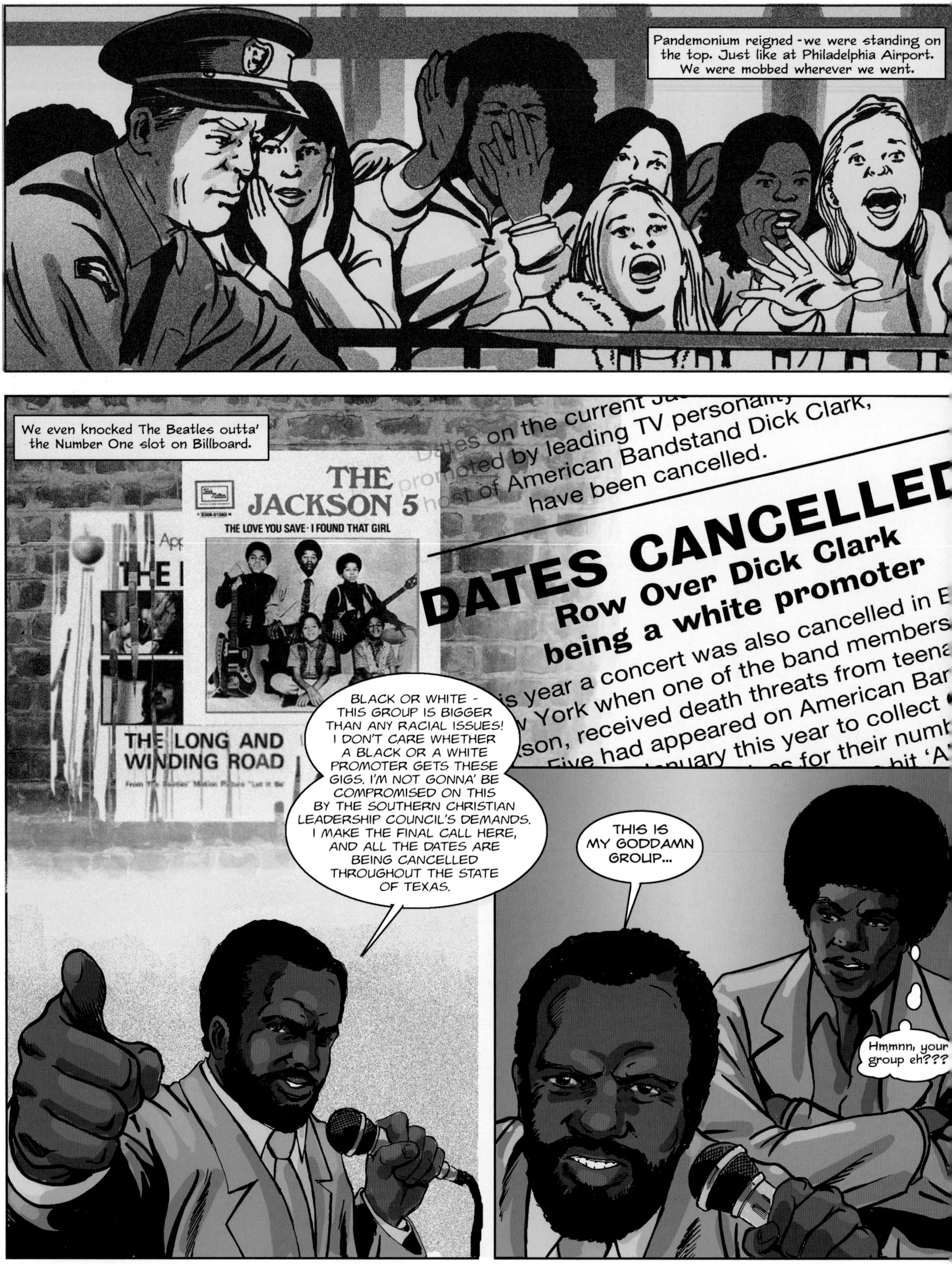

Pandemonium reigned - we were standing on the top. Just like at Philadelphia Airport. We were mobbed wherever we went.
We even knocked The Beatles outta' the Number One slot on Billboard.
THE JACKSON 5
THE LOVE YOU SAVE · I FOUND THAT GIRL
THE LONG AND WINDING ROAD
Dates on the current
promoted by leading TV
host of American Bandstand Dick Clark,
have been cancelled.
DATES CANCELLED
Row Over Dick Clark
being a white promoter
year a concert was also cancelled in
York when one of the band members
received death threats from
Five had appeared on American
this year to collect
BLACK OR WHITE - THIS GROUP IS BIGGER THAN ANY RACIAL ISSUES! I DON'T CARE WHETHER A BLACK OR A WHITE PROMOTER GETS THESE GIGS. I'M NOT GONNA' BE COMPROMISED ON THIS BY THE SOUTHERN CHRISTIAN LEADERSHIP COUNCIL'S DEMANDS. I MAKE THE FINAL CALL HERE, AND ALL THE DATES ARE BEING CANCELLED THROUGHOUT THE STATE OF TEXAS.
THIS IS MY GODDAMN GROUP...
Hmmnn, your group eh???

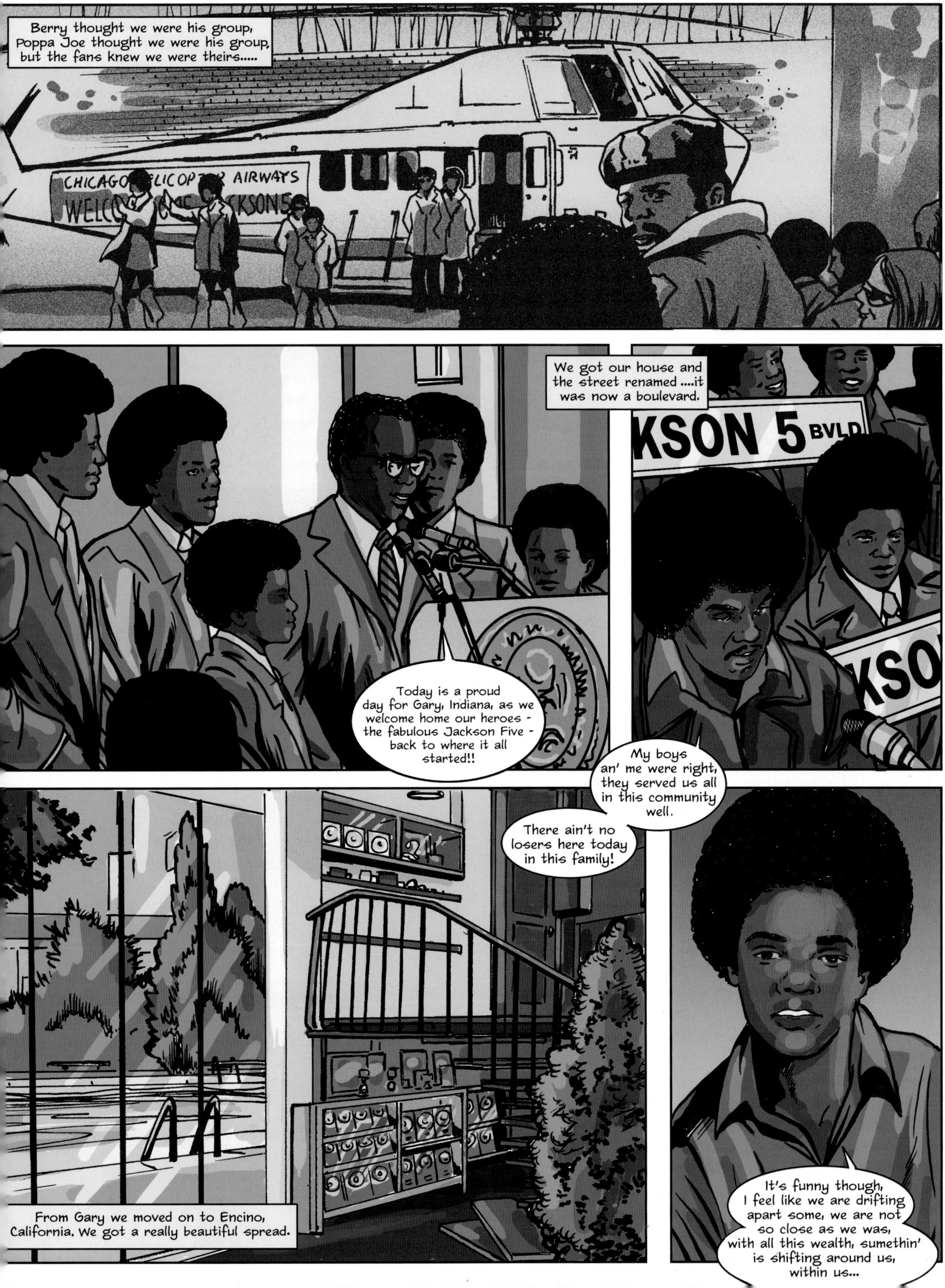
Berry thought we were his group, Poppa Joe thought we were his group, but the fans knew we were theirs.....
Today is a proud day for Gary, Indiana, as we welcome home our heroes - the fabulous Jackson Five - back to where it all started!!
We got our house and the street renamed ....it was now a boulevard.
KSON 5 BVLD
My boys an' me were right, they served us all in this community well.
There ain't no losers here today in this family!
From Gary we moved on to Encino, California. We got a really beautiful spread.
It's funny though, I feel like we are drifting apart some, we are not so close as we was, with all this wealth, sumethin' is shifting around us, within us...

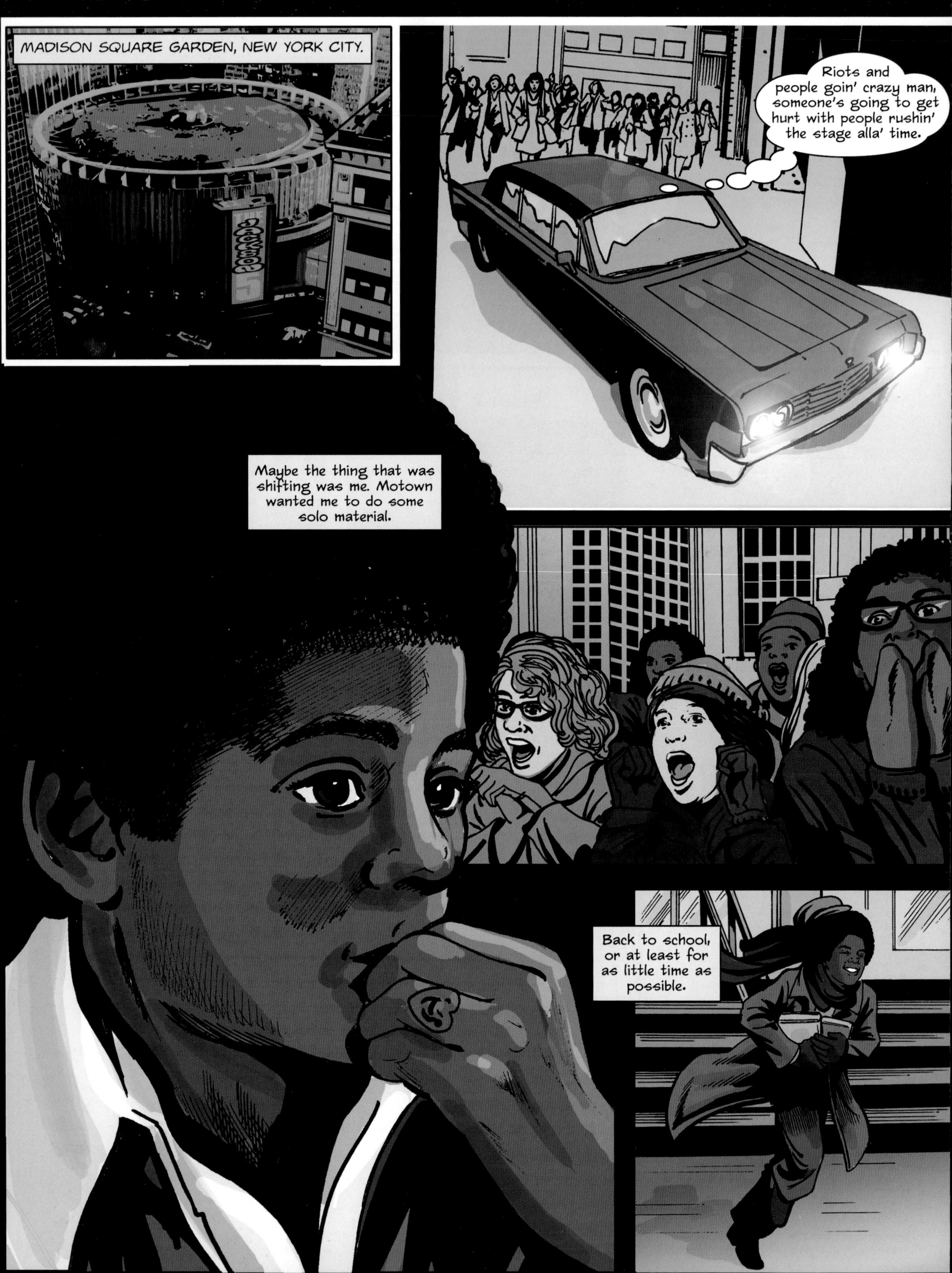
MADISON SQUARE GARDEN, NEW YORK CITY.
Riots and people goin' crazy man, someone's going to get hurt with people rushin' the stage alla' time.
Maybe the thing that was shifting was me. Motown wanted me to do some solo material.
Back to school, or at least for as little time as possible.

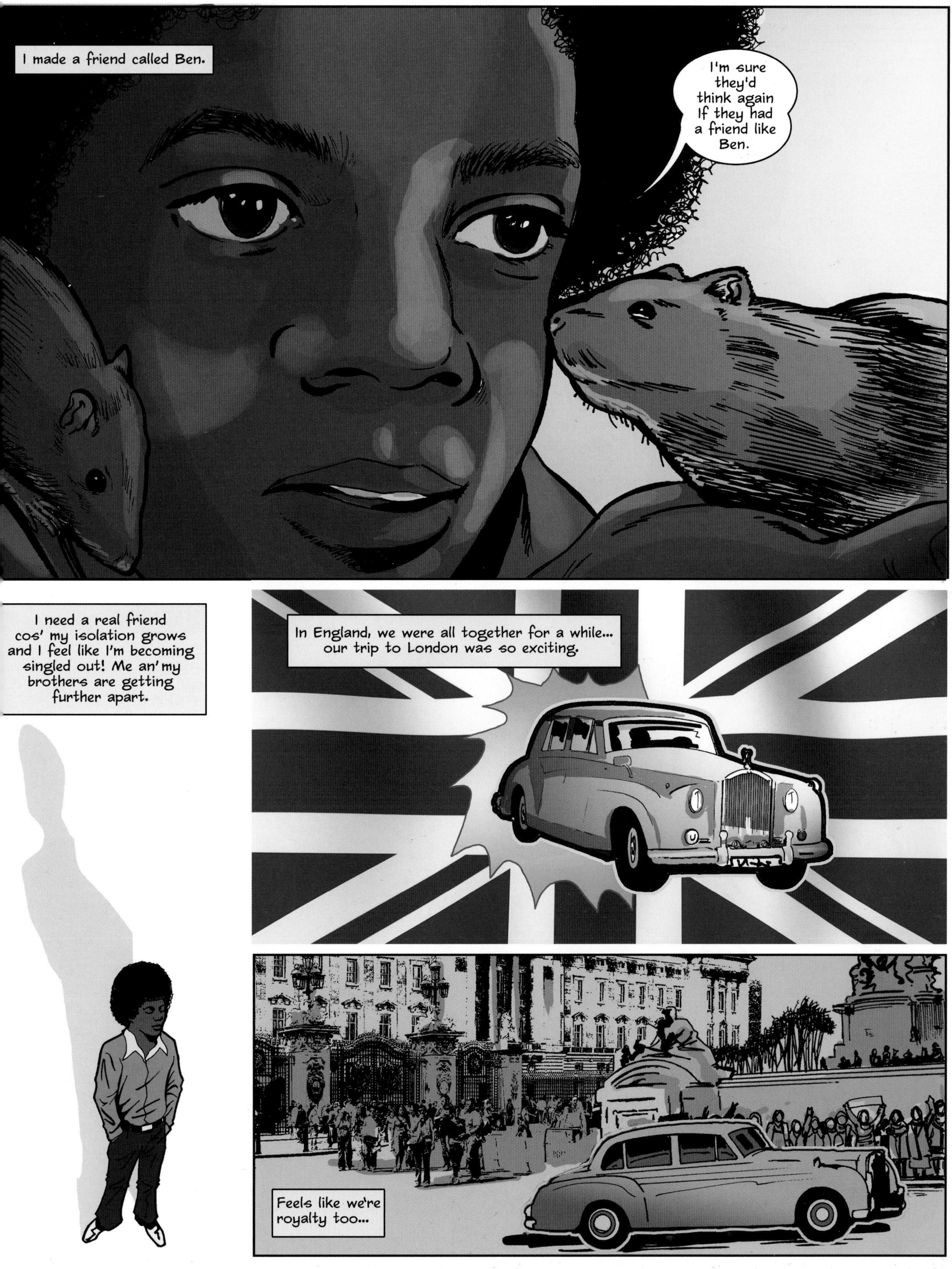

I made a friend called Ben.
I'm sure they'd think again If they had a friend like Ben.
I need a real friend cos' my isolation grows and I feel like I'm becoming singled out! Me an' my brothers are getting further apart.
In England, we were all together for a while... our trip to London was so exciting.
Feels like we're royalty too...

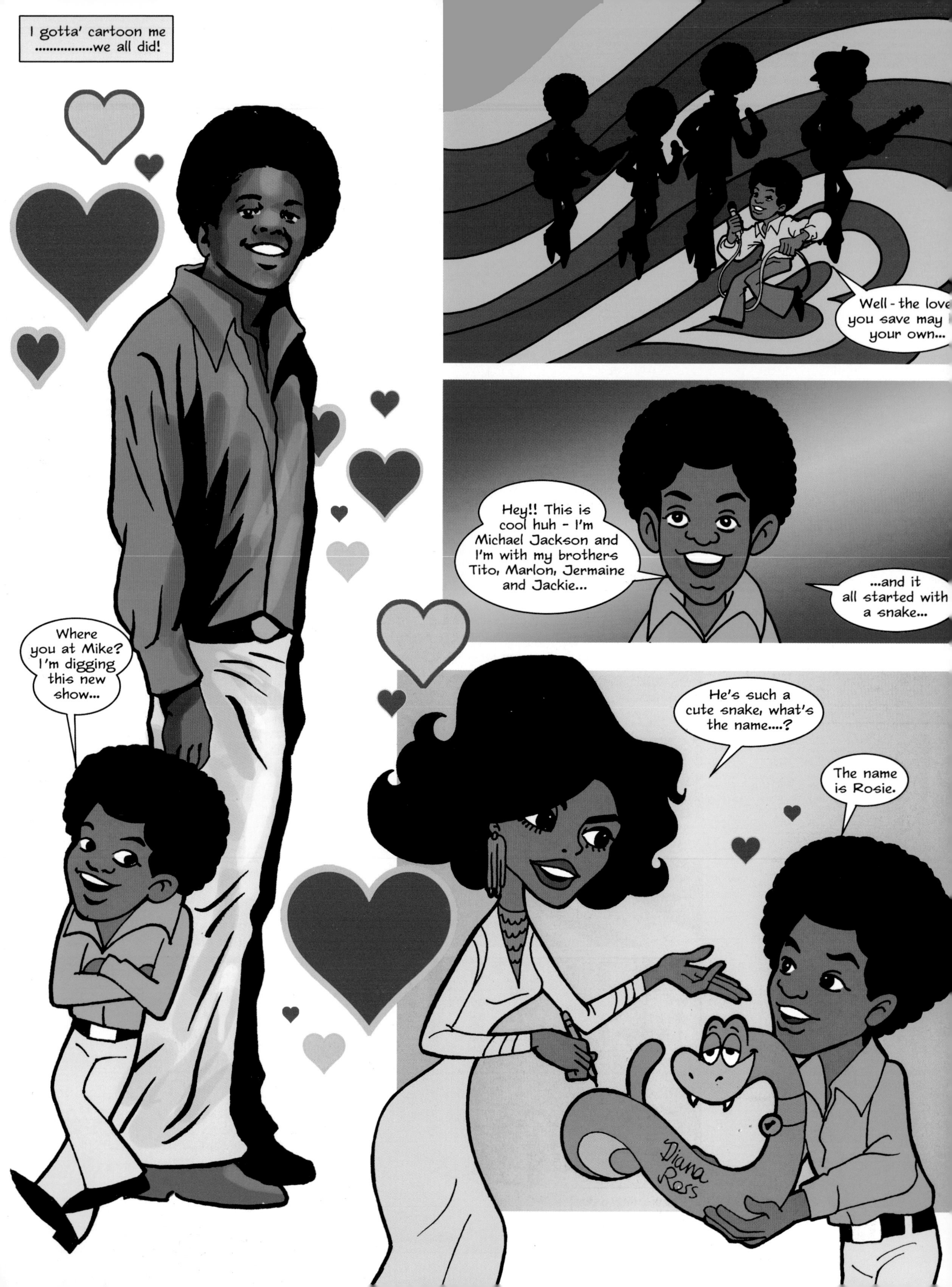
I gotta' cartoon me
................we all did!
Where you at Mike? I'm digging this new show...
Well - the love you save may your own...
Hey!! This is cool huh - I'm Michael Jackson and I'm with my brothers Tito, Marlon, Jermaine and Jackie...
...and it all started with a snake...
He's such a cute snake, what's the name....?
The name is Rosie.
Diana Ross

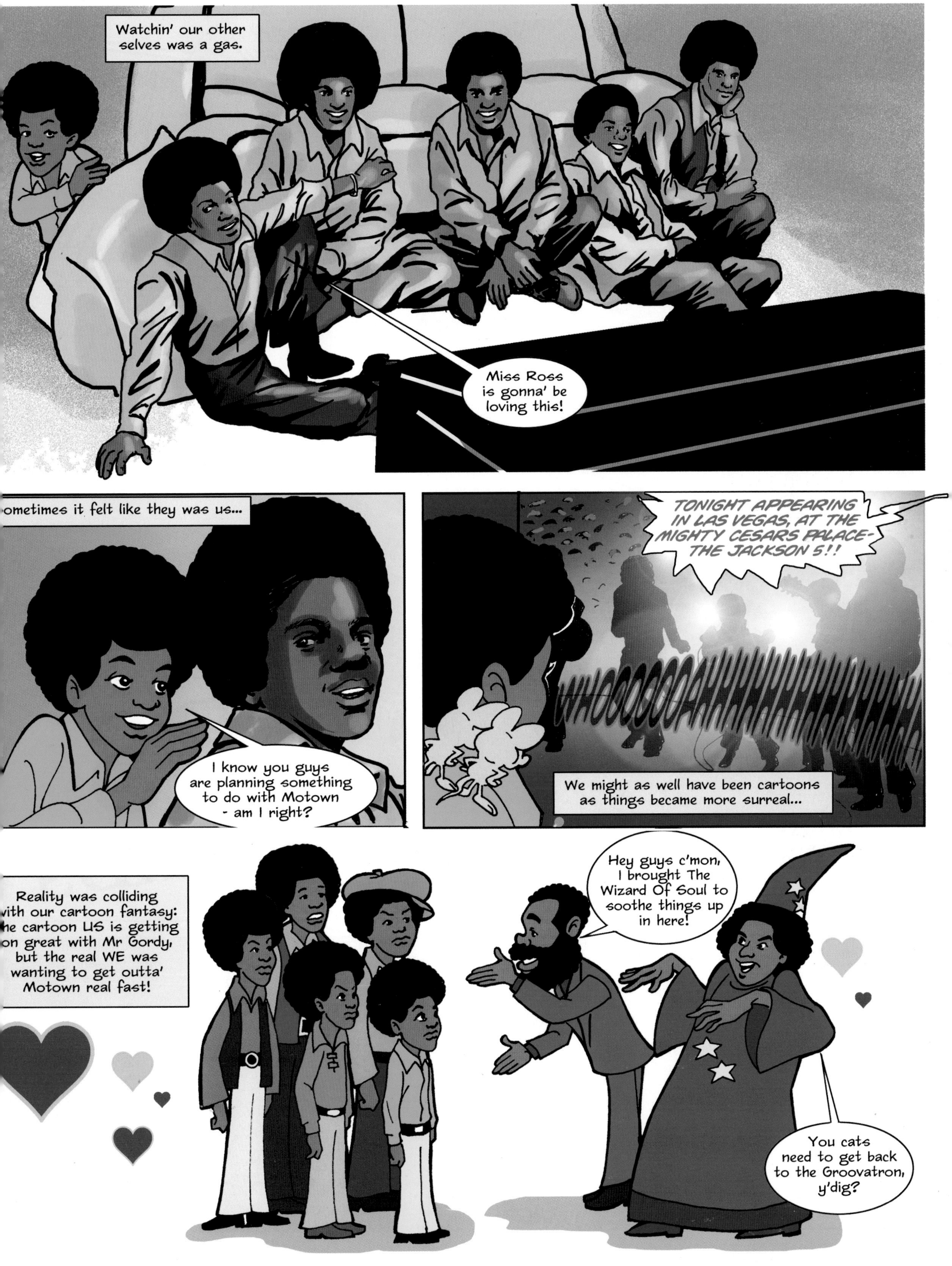

Watchin' our other selves was a gas.
Miss Ross is gonna' be loving this!
ometimes it felt like they was us...
I know you guys are planning something to do with Motown - am I right?
TONIGHT APPEARING IN LAS VEGAS, AT THE MIGHTY CESARS PALACE- THE JACKSON 5!!
WHOOOOOOAHHHHHHHHHHHHHHH
We might as well have been cartoons as things became more surreal...
Reality was colliding with our cartoon fantasy: he cartoon US is getting on great with Mr Gordy, but the real WE was wanting to get outta' Motown real fast!
Hey guys c'mon, I brought The Wizard Of Soul to soothe things up in here!
You cats need to get back to the Groovatron, y'dig?

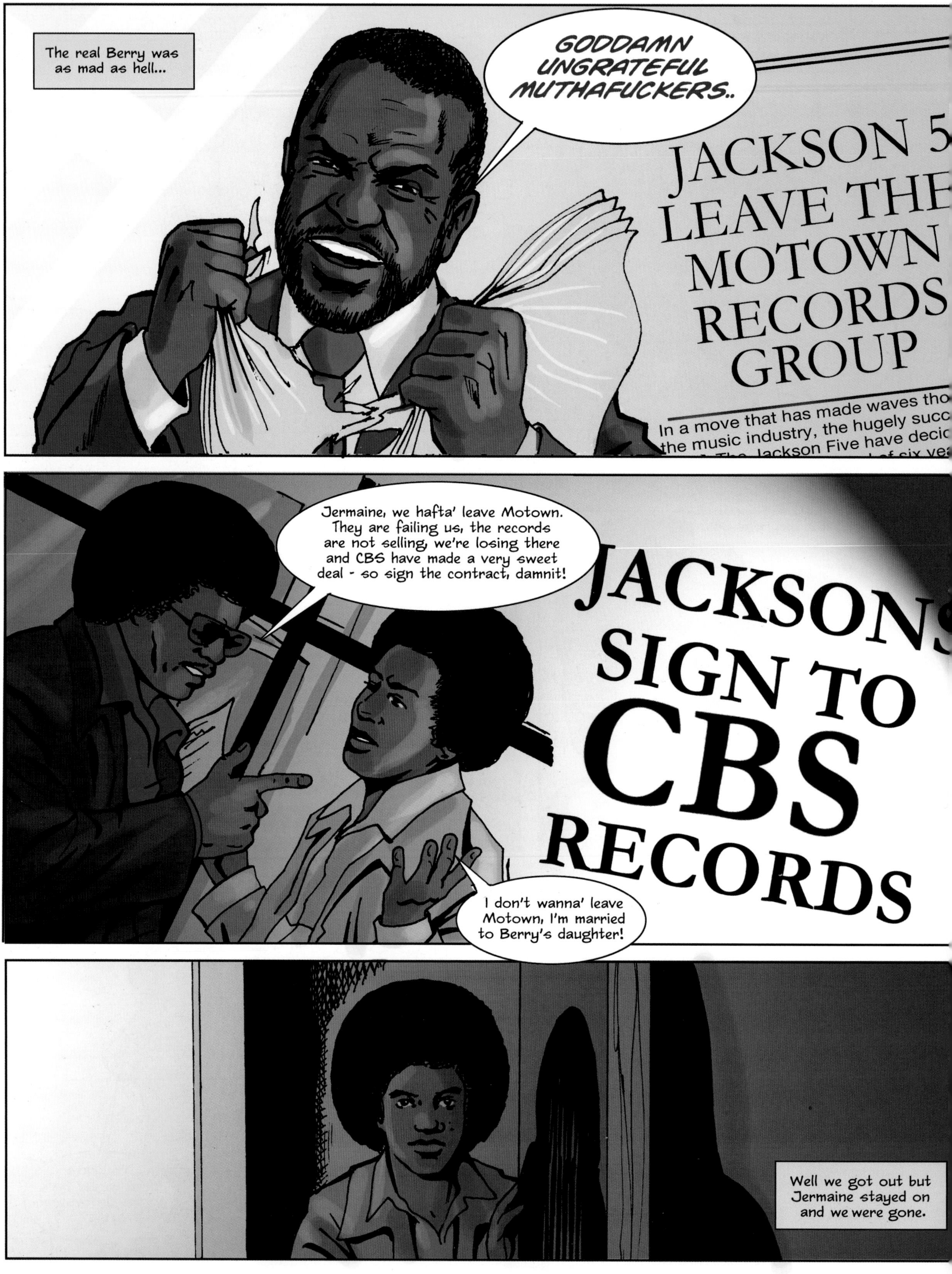

The real Berry was as mad as hell...
GODDAMN UNGRATEFUL MUTHAFUCKERS..
JACKSON 5 LEAVE THE MOTOWN RECORDS GROUP
In a move that has made waves tho
the music industry, the hugely succ
Jermaine, we hafta' leave Motown. They are failing us, the records are not selling, we're losing there and CBS have made a very sweet deal - so sign the contract, damnit!
JACKSONS SIGN TO CBS RECORDS
I don't wanna' leave Motown, I'm married to Berry's daughter!
Well we got out but Jermaine stayed on and we were gone.

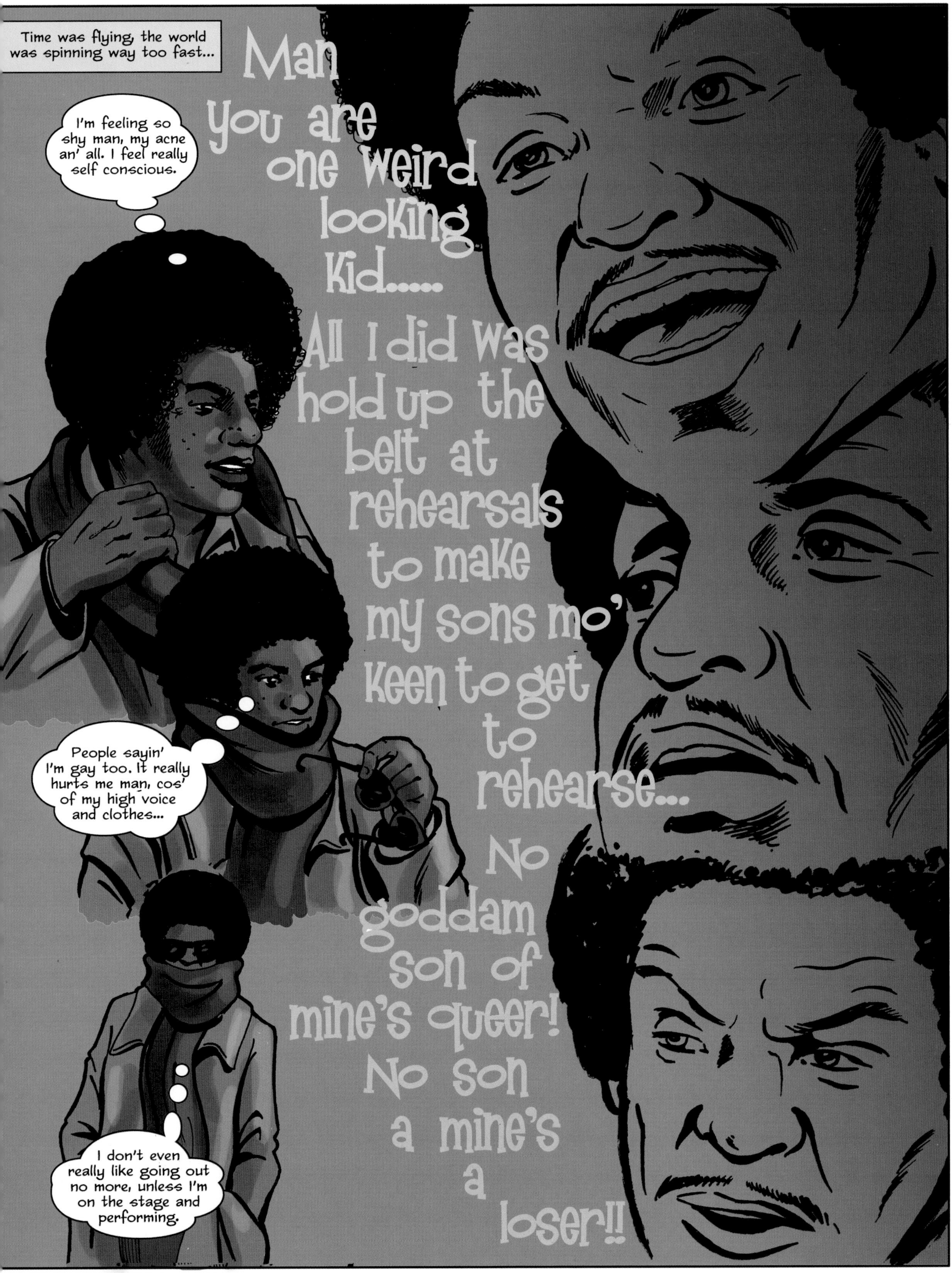
Time was flying, the world was spinning way too fast...
I'm feeling so shy man, my acne an' all. I feel really self conscious.
Man you are one weird looking kid..... All I did was hold up the belt at rehearsals to make my sons mo' keen to get to rehearse... No goddam son of mine's queer! No son a mine's a loser!!
People sayin' I'm gay too. It really hurts me man, cos' of my high voice and clothes...
I don't even really like going out no more, unless I'm on the stage and performing.

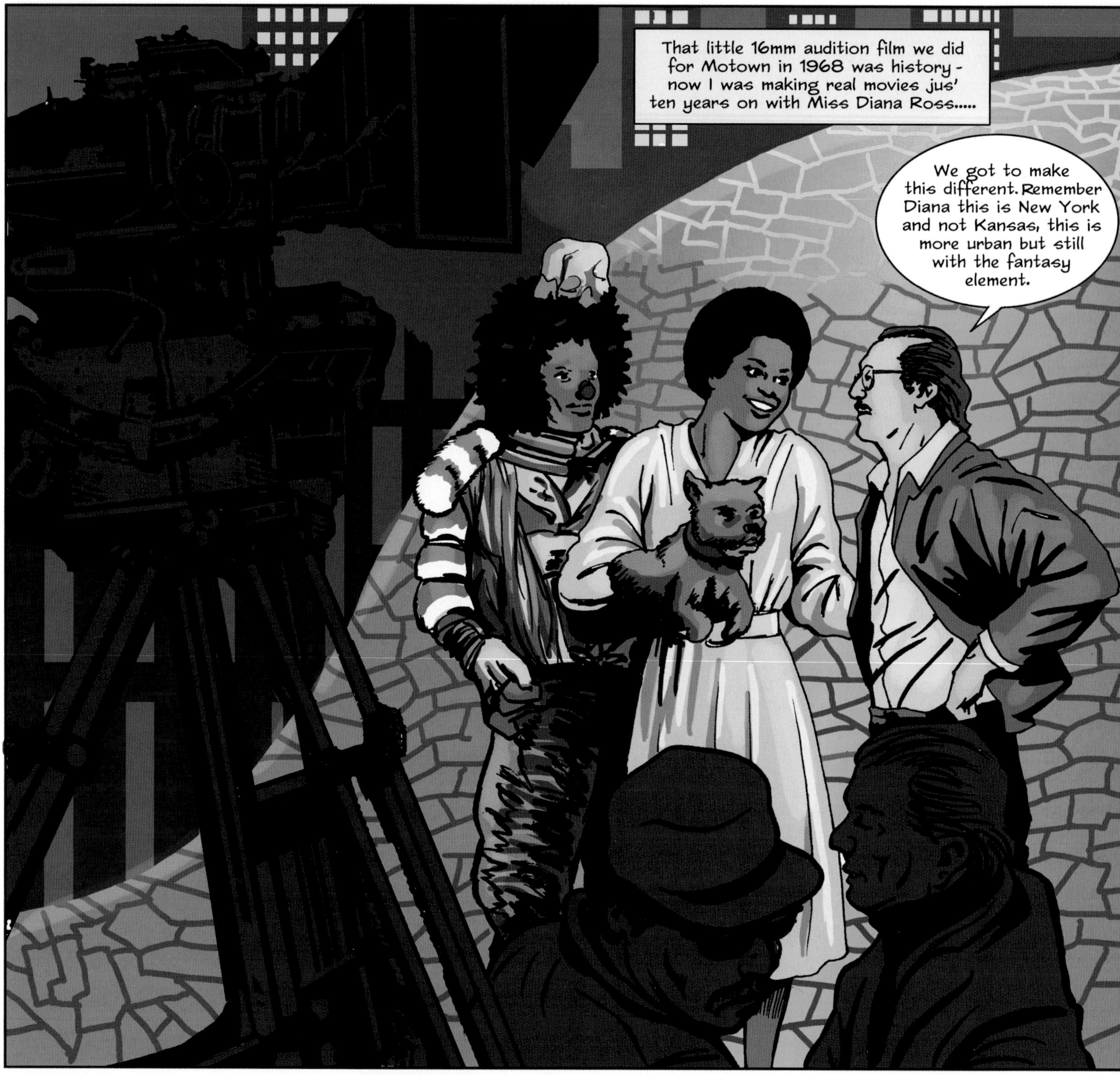
That little 16mm audition film we did for Motown in 1968 was history - now I was making real movies jus' ten years on with Miss Diana Ross.....
We got to make this different. Remember Diana this is New York and not Kansas, this is more urban but still with the fantasy element.

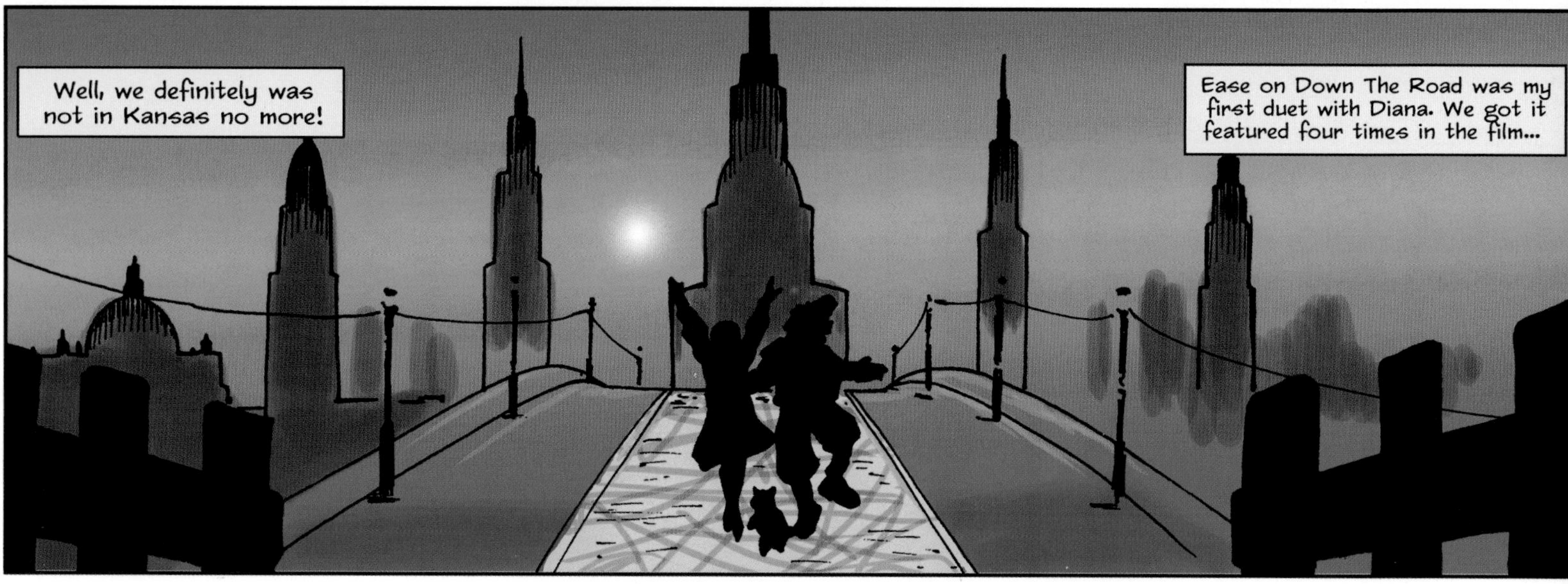
Well, we definitely was not in Kansas no more!
Ease on Down The Road was my first duet with Diana. We got it featured four times in the film...

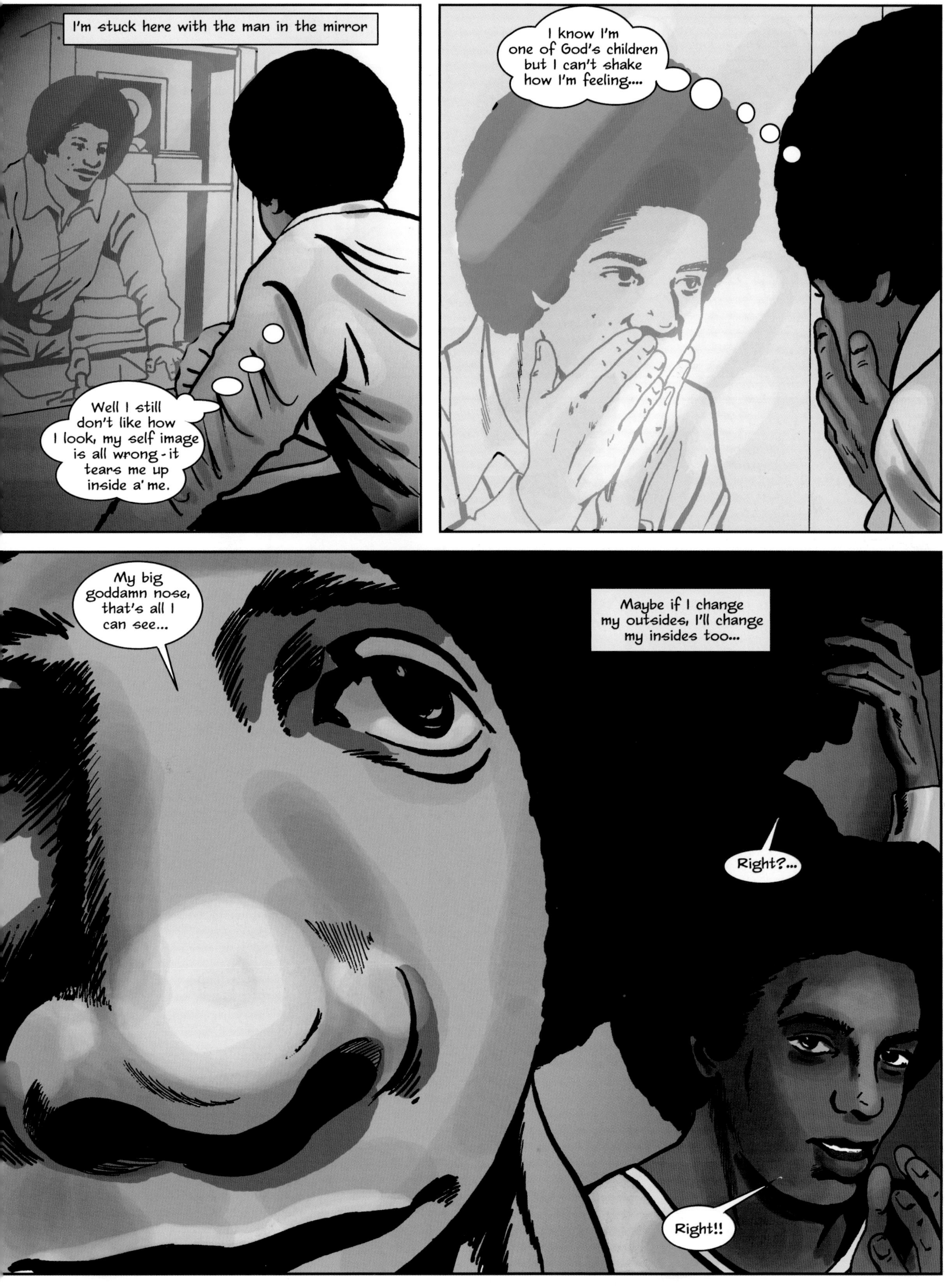
I'm stuck here with the man in the mirror
Well I still don't like how I look, my self image is all wrong - it tears me up inside a' me.
I know I'm one of God's children but I can't shake how I'm feeling....
My big goddamn nose, that's all I can see...
Maybe if I change my outsides, I'll change my insides too...
Right?...
Right!!

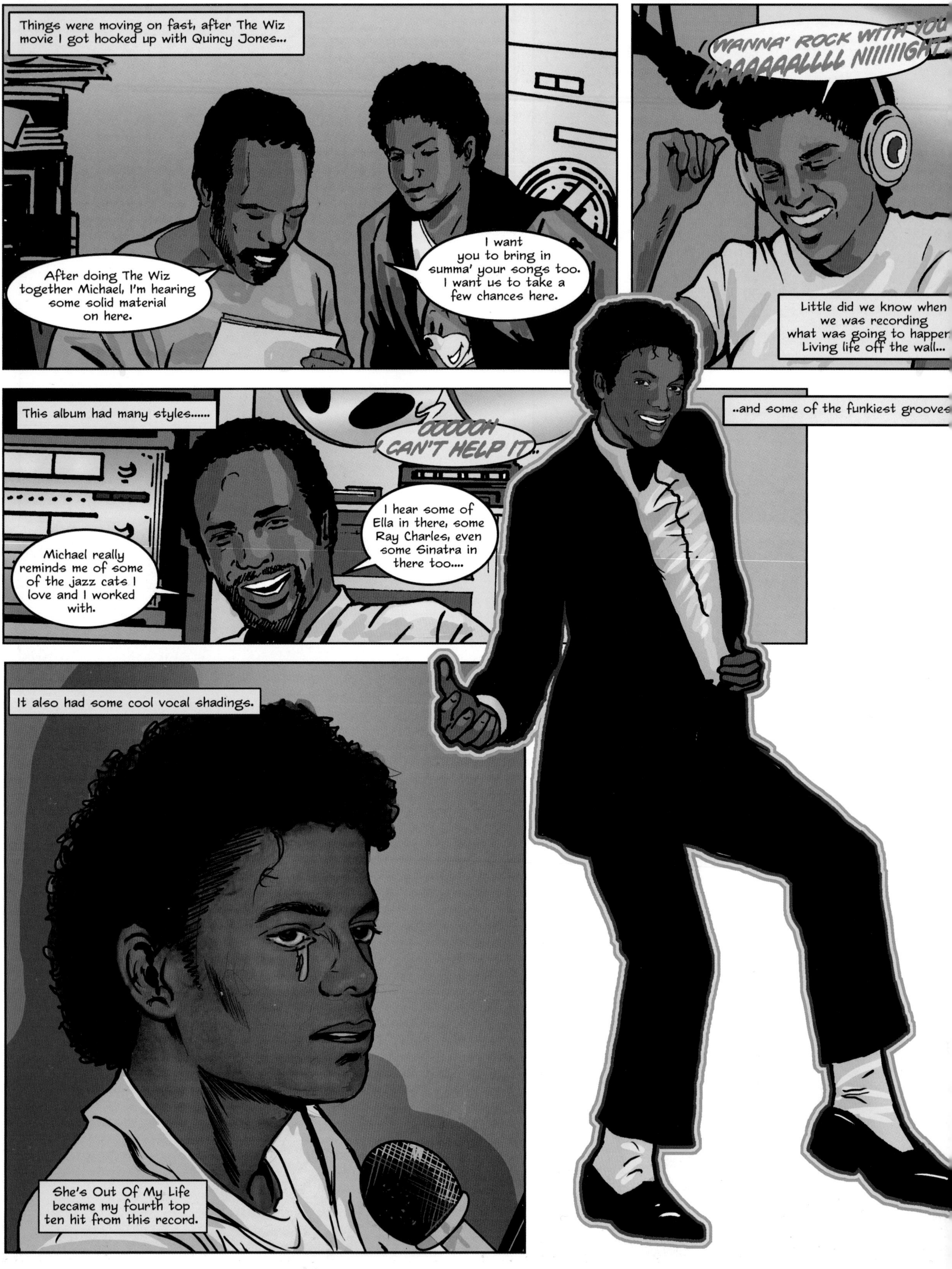

Things were moving on fast, after The Wiz movie I got hooked up with Quincy Jones...
After doing The Wiz together Michael, I'm hearing some solid material on here.
I want you to bring in summa' your songs too. I want us to take a few chances here.
I WANNA' ROCK WITH YOU AAAAAAALLLL NIIIIIIGHT...
Little did we know when we was recording what was going to happen Living life off the wall...
This album had many styles......
OOOOOH I CAN'T HELP IT...
Michael really reminds me of some of the jazz cats I love and I worked with.
I hear some of Ella in there, some Ray Charles, even some Sinatra in there too....
..and some of the funkiest grooves
It also had some cool vocal shadings.
She's Out Of My Life became my fourth top ten hit from this record.

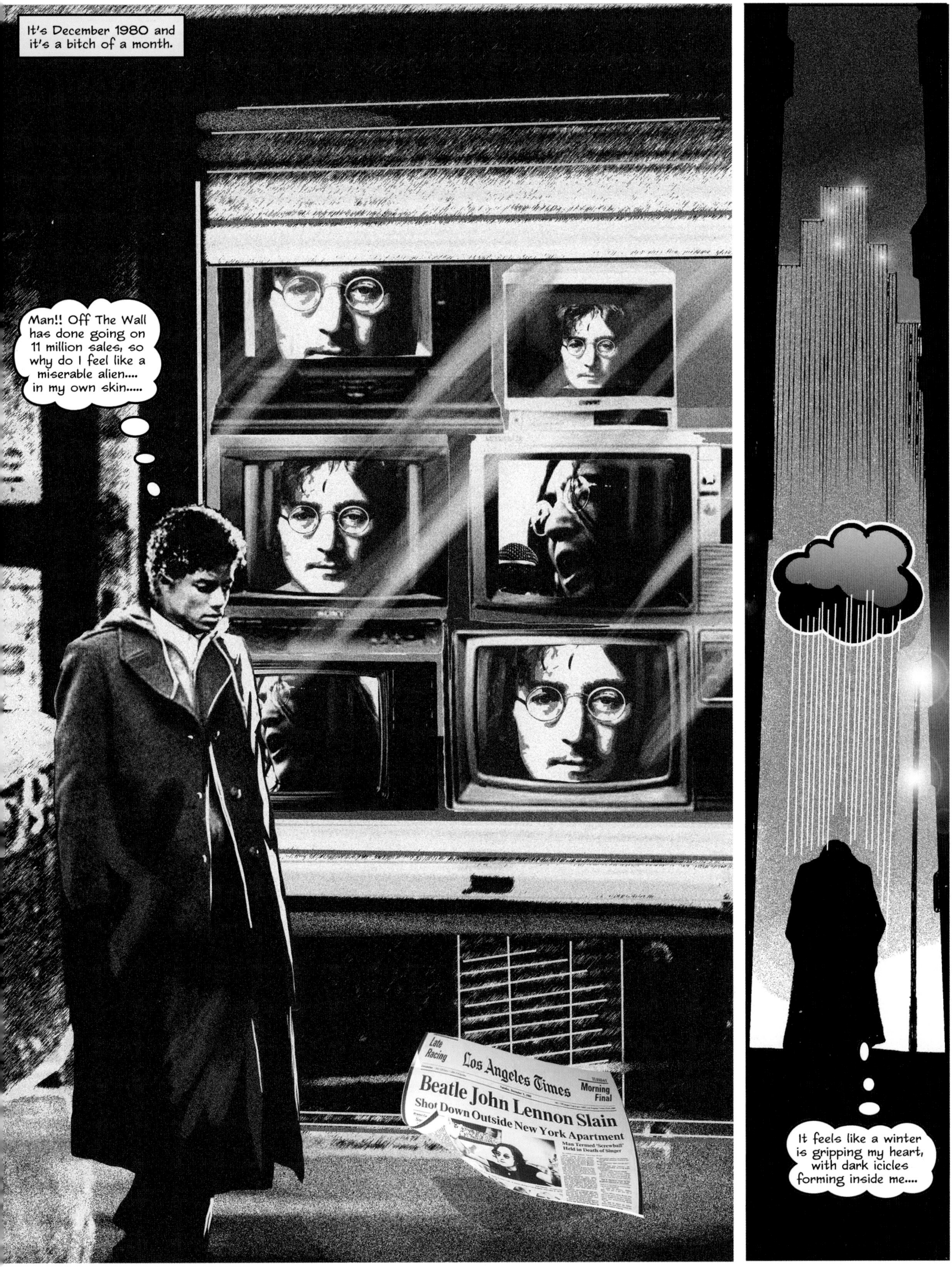
It's December 1980 and it's a bitch of a month.
Man!! Off The Wall has done going on 11 million sales, so why do I feel like a miserable alien.... in my own skin.....
Late Racing
Los Angeles Times
Tuesday
Morning Final
Beatle John Lennon Slain
Shot Down Outside New York Apartment
Man Termed 'Screwball' Held in Death of Singer
It feels like a winter is gripping my heart, with dark icicles forming inside me....

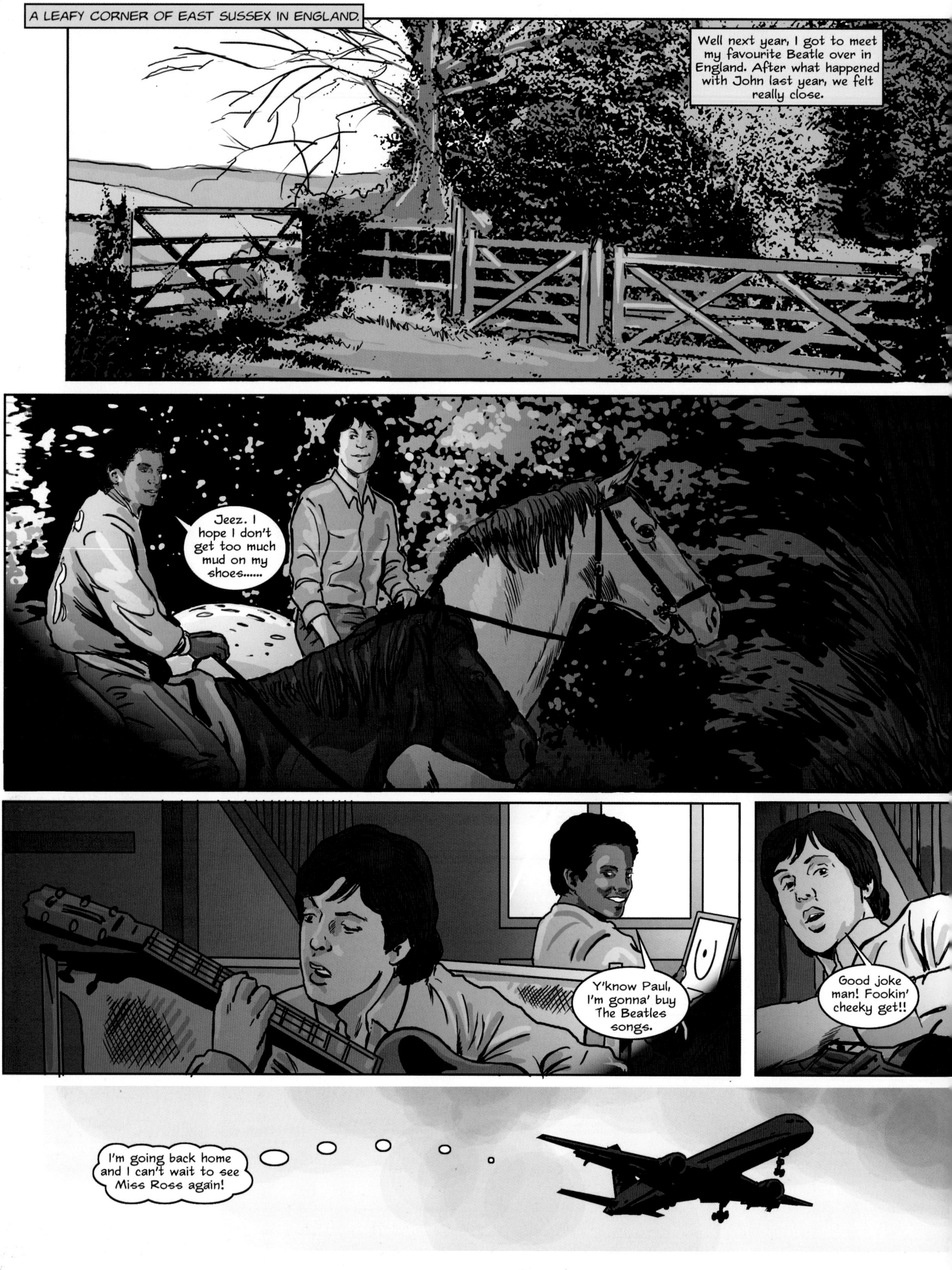
A LEAFY CORNER OF EAST SUSSEX IN ENGLAND.
Well next year, I got to meet my favourite Beatle over in England. After what happened with John last year, we felt really close.
Jeez. I hope I don't get too much mud on my shoes......
Y'know Paul, I'm gonna' buy The Beatles songs.
Good joke man! Fookin' cheeky get!!
I'm going back home and I can't wait to see Miss Ross again!

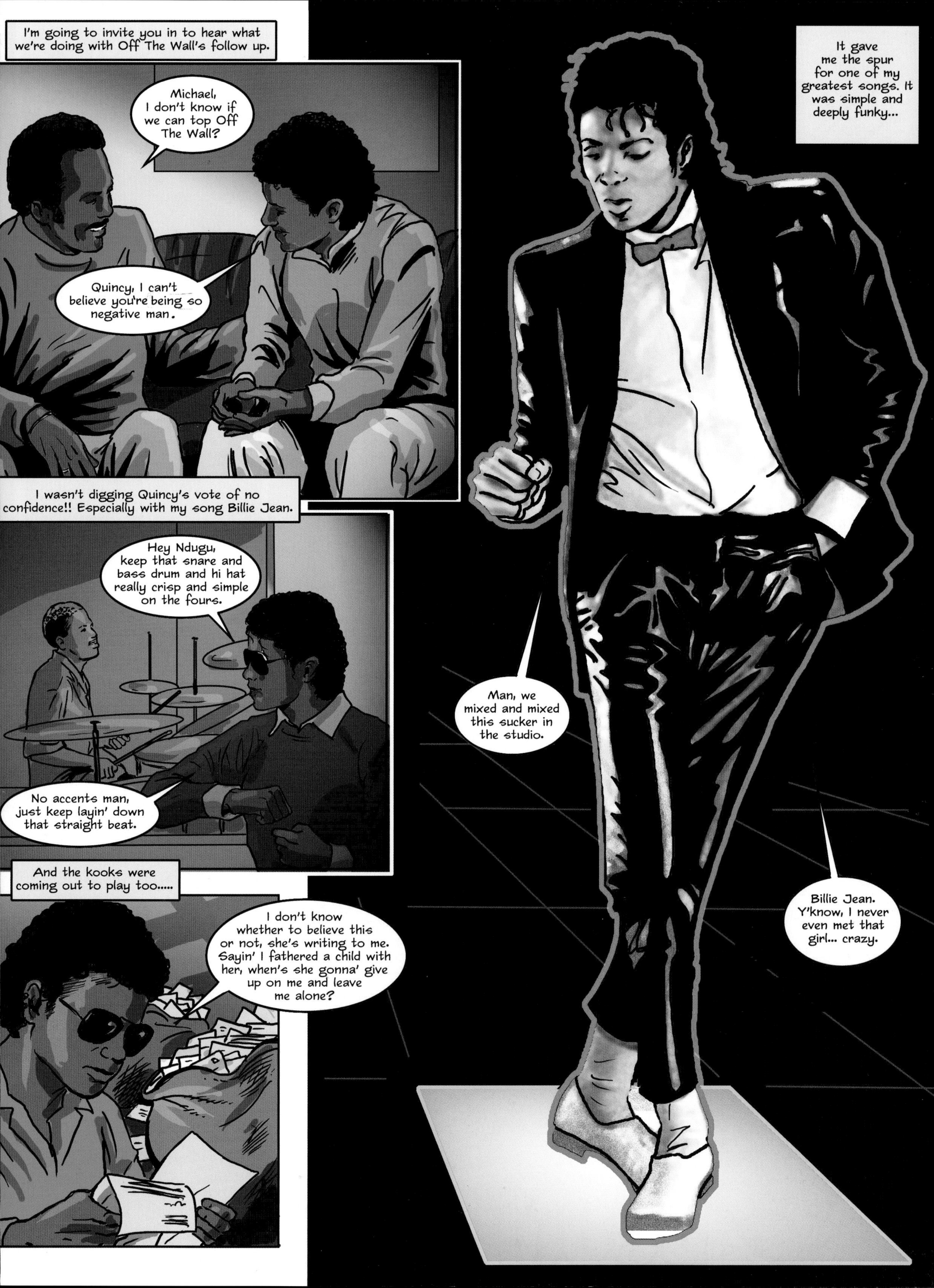
I'm going to invite you in to hear what we're doing with Off The Wall's follow up.
Michael, I don't know if we can top Off The Wall?
Quincy, I can't believe you're being so negative man.
I wasn't digging Quincy's vote of no confidence!! Especially with my song Billie Jean.
Hey Ndugu, keep that snare and bass drum and hi hat really crisp and simple on the fours.
No accents man, just keep layin' down that straight beat.
And the kooks were coming out to play too.....
I don't know whether to believe this or not, she's writing to me. Sayin' I fathered a child with her, when's she gonna' give up on me and leave me alone?
It gave me the spur for one of my greatest songs. It was simple and deeply funky...
Man, we mixed and mixed this sucker in the studio.
Billie Jean. Y'know, I never even met that girl... crazy.

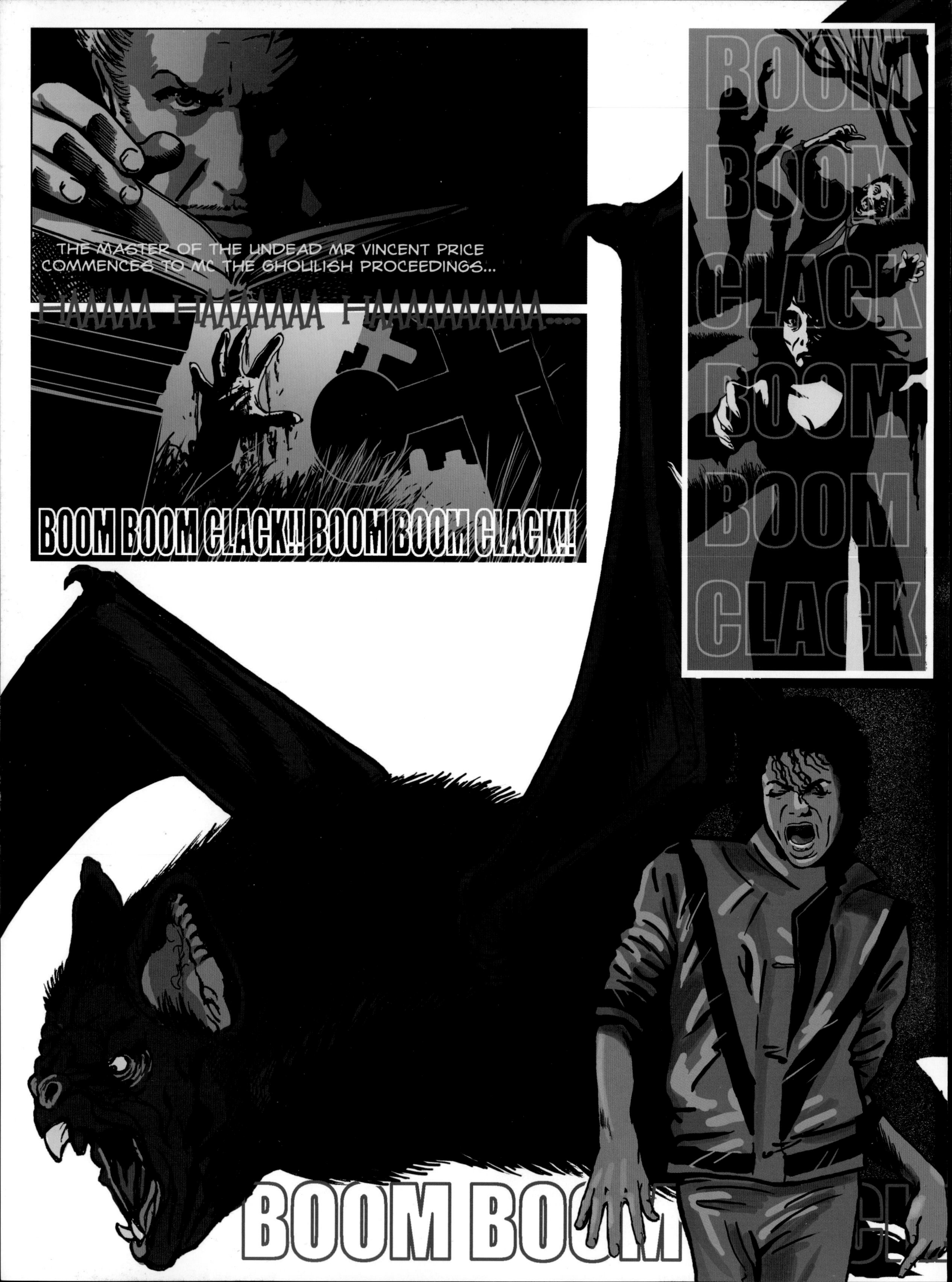
THE MASTER OF THE UNDEAD MR VINCENT PRICE COMMENCES TO MC THE GHOULISH PROCEEDINGS...
HAAAAAA HAAAAAAAA HAAAAAAAAAAA....
BOOM BOOM CLACK!! BOOM BOOM CLACK!!
BOOM BOOM CLACK BOOM BOOM CLACK
BOOM BOOM

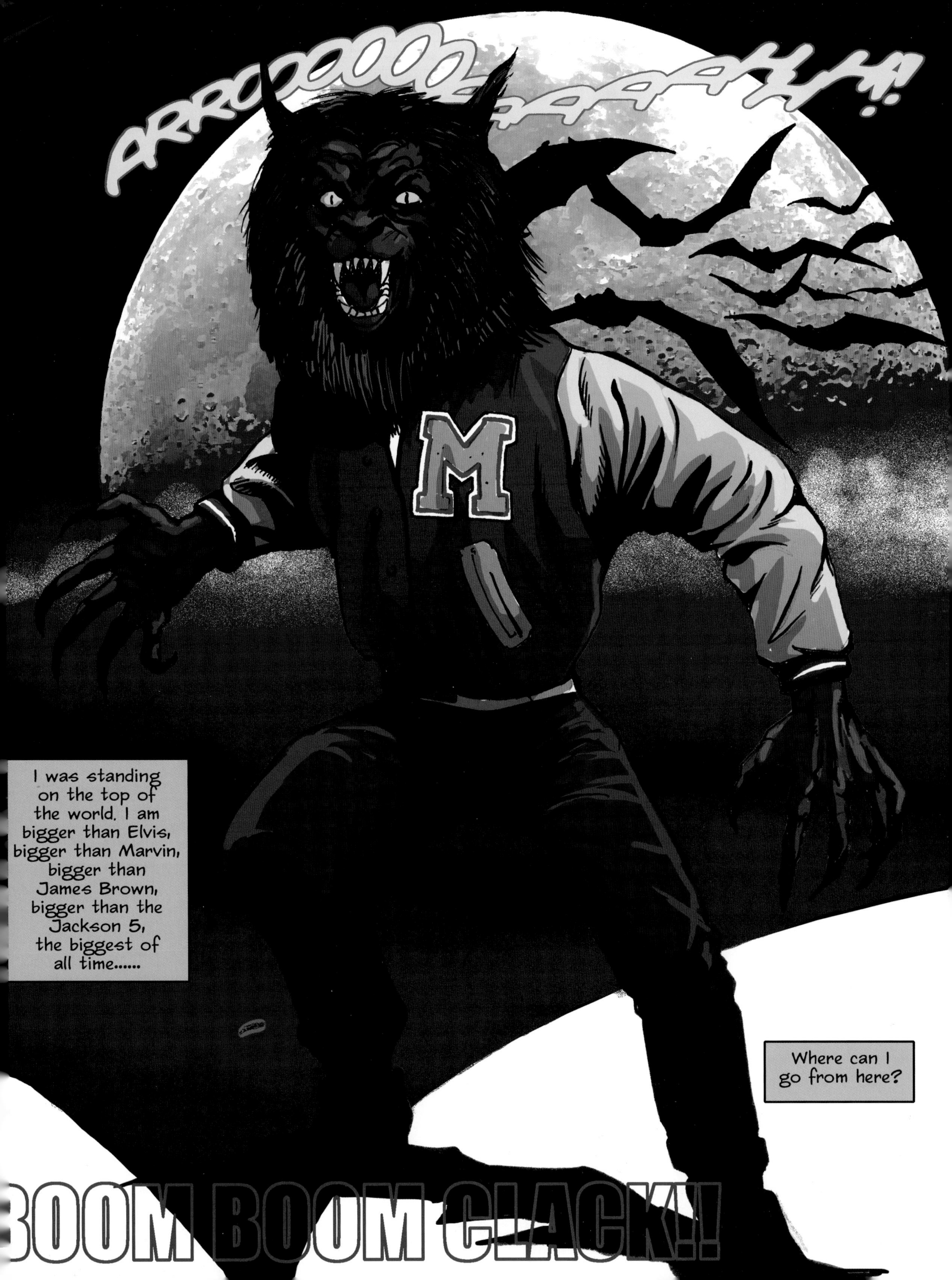
ARROOOOOOAAAAAHH!!
I was standing on the top of the world. I am bigger than Elvis, bigger than Marvin, bigger than James Brown, bigger than the Jackson 5, the biggest of all time......
Where can I go from here?
BOOM BOOM CLACK!!

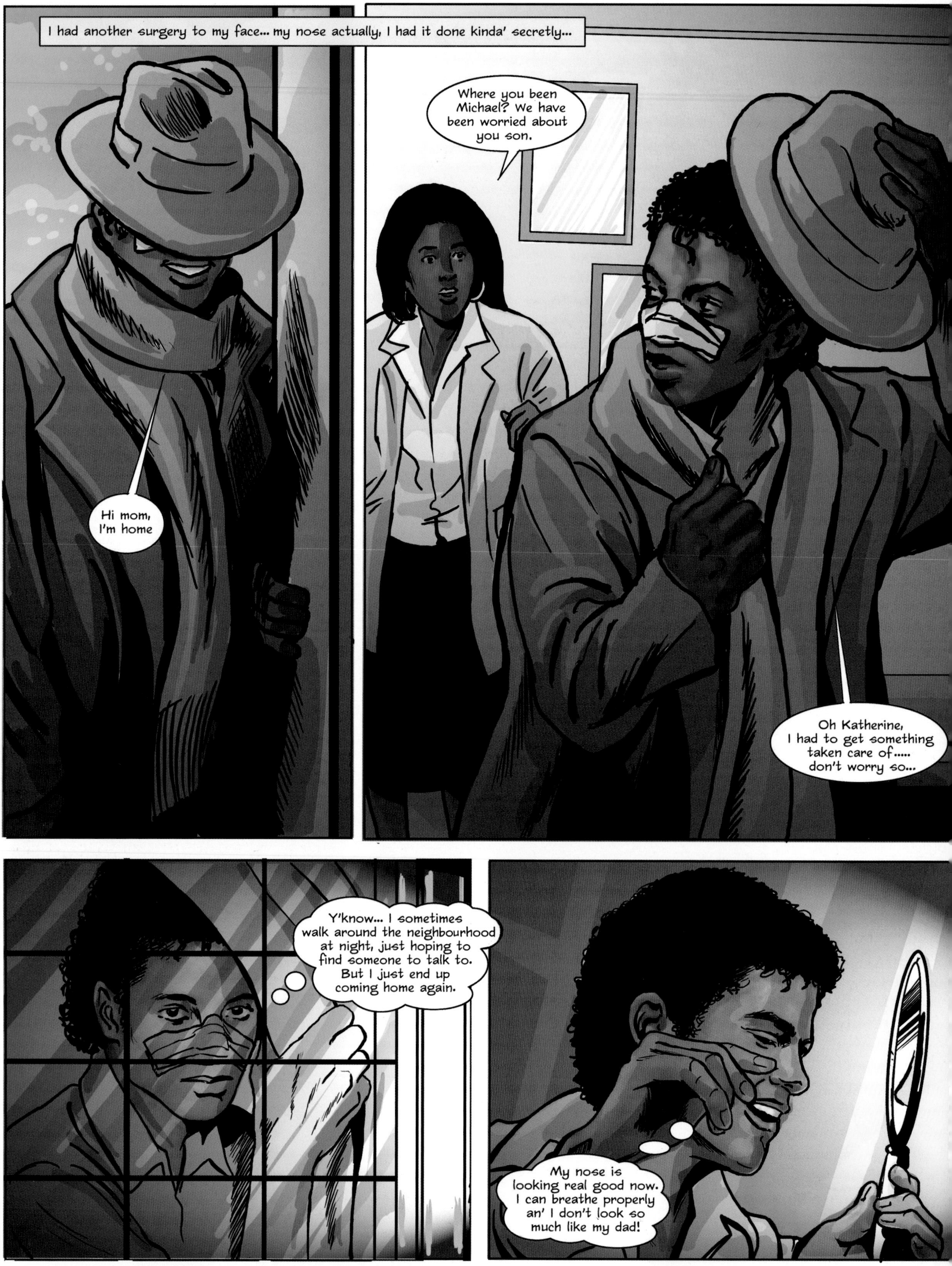
I had another surgery to my face... my nose actually, I had it done kinda' secretly...
Hi mom, I'm home
Where you been Michael? We have been worried about you son.
Oh Katherine, I had to get something taken care of..... don't worry so...
Y'know... I sometimes walk around the neighbourhood at night, just hoping to find someone to talk to. But I just end up coming home again.
My nose is looking real good now. I can breathe properly an' I don't look so much like my dad!

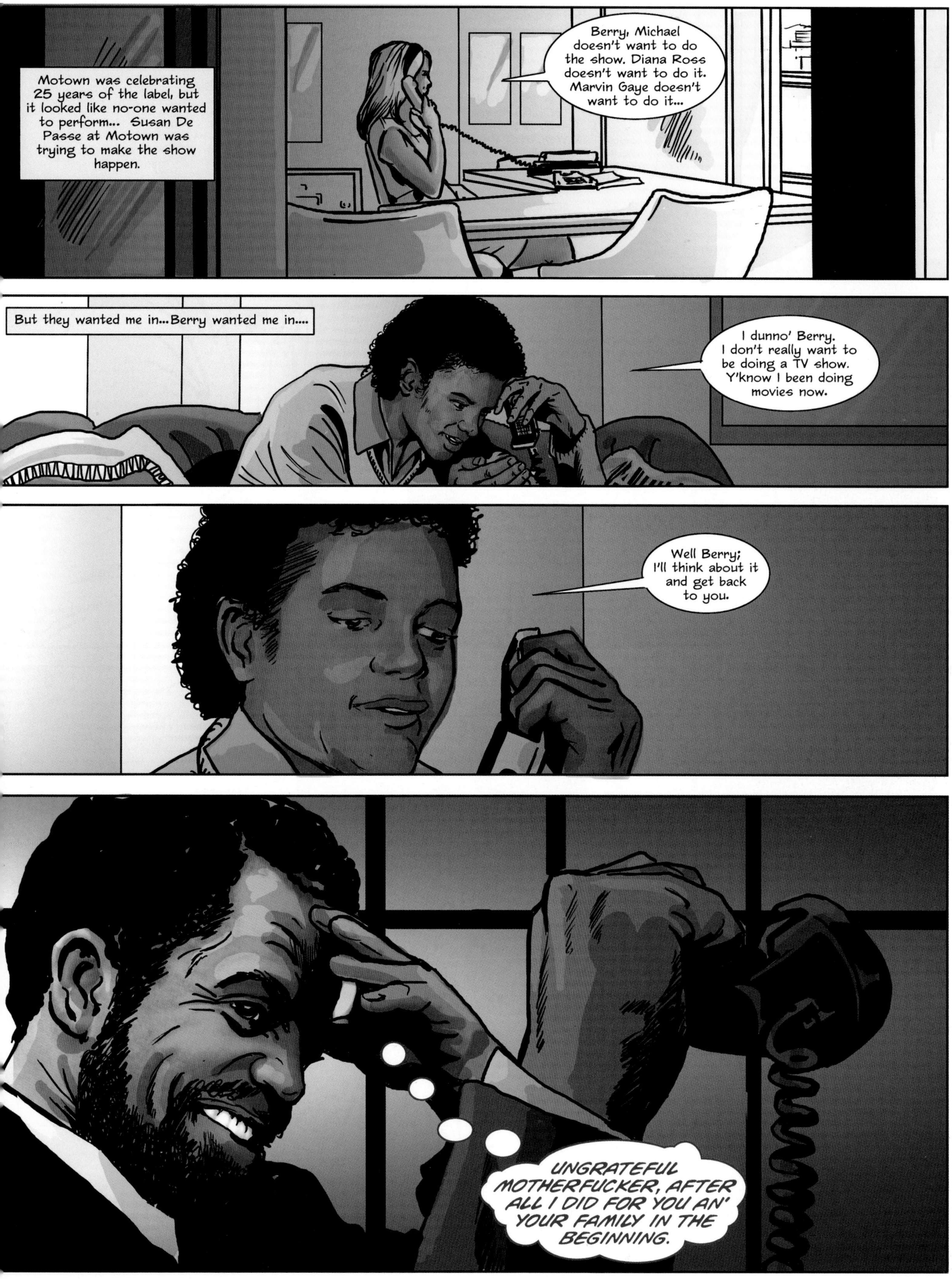
Motown was celebrating 25 years of the label, but it looked like no-one wanted to perform... Susan De Passe at Motown was trying to make the show happen.
Berry, Michael doesn't want to do the show. Diana Ross doesn't want to do it. Marvin Gaye doesn't want to do it...
But they wanted me in...Berry wanted me in....
I dunno' Berry. I don't really want to be doing a TV show. Y'know I been doing movies now.
Well Berry; I'll think about it and get back to you.
UNGRATEFUL MOTHERFUCKER, AFTER ALL I DID FOR YOU AN' YOUR FAMILY IN THE BEGINNING.

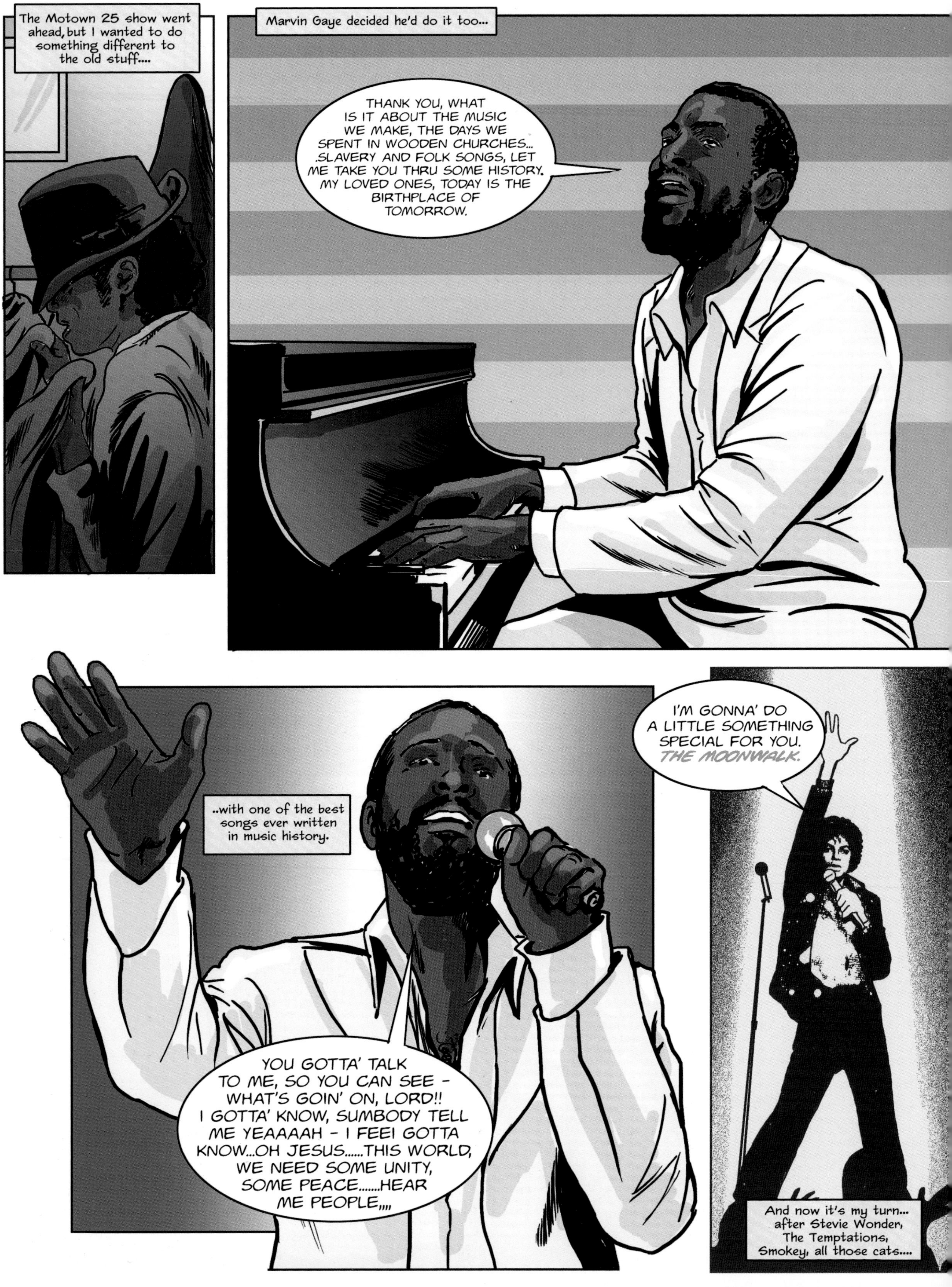
The Motown 25 show went ahead, but I wanted to do something different to the old stuff....
Marvin Gaye decided he'd do it too...
THANK YOU, WHAT IS IT ABOUT THE MUSIC WE MAKE, THE DAYS WE SPENT IN WOODEN CHURCHES... .SLAVERY AND FOLK SONGS, LET ME TAKE YOU THRU SOME HISTORY. MY LOVED ONES, TODAY IS THE BIRTHPLACE OF TOMORROW.
..with one of the best songs ever written in music history.
YOU GOTTA' TALK TO ME, SO YOU CAN SEE - WHAT'S GOIN' ON, LORD!! I GOTTA' KNOW, SUMBODY TELL ME YEAAAAH - I FEEI GOTTA KNOW...OH JESUS......THIS WORLD, WE NEED SOME UNITY, SOME PEACE.......HEAR ME PEOPLE,,,,
I'M GONNA' DO A LITTLE SOMETHING SPECIAL FOR YOU. THE MOONWALK.
And now it's my turn... after Stevie Wonder, The Temptations, Smokey, all those cats....

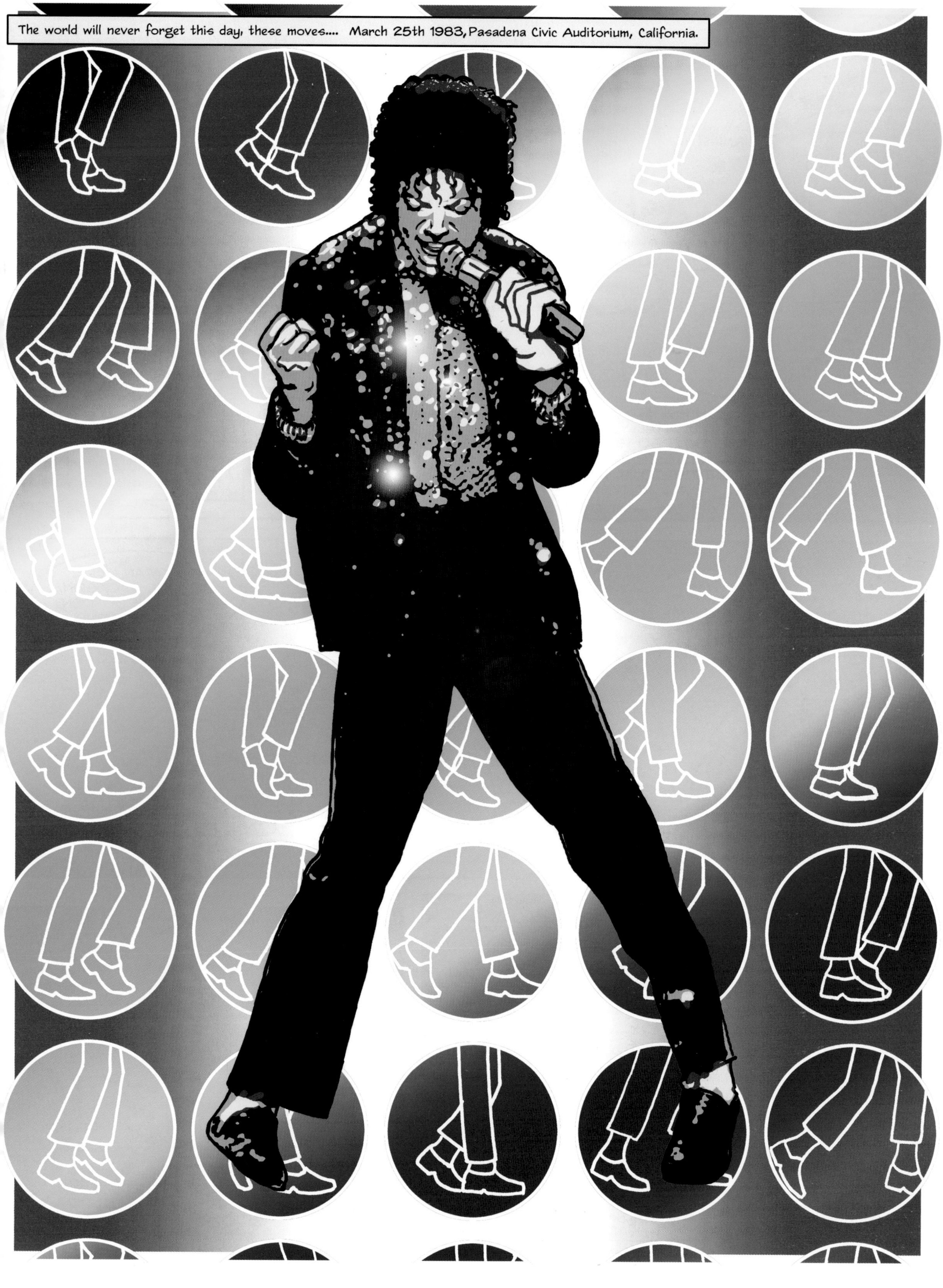
The world will never forget this day, these moves.... March 25th 1983, Pasadena Civic Auditorium, California.

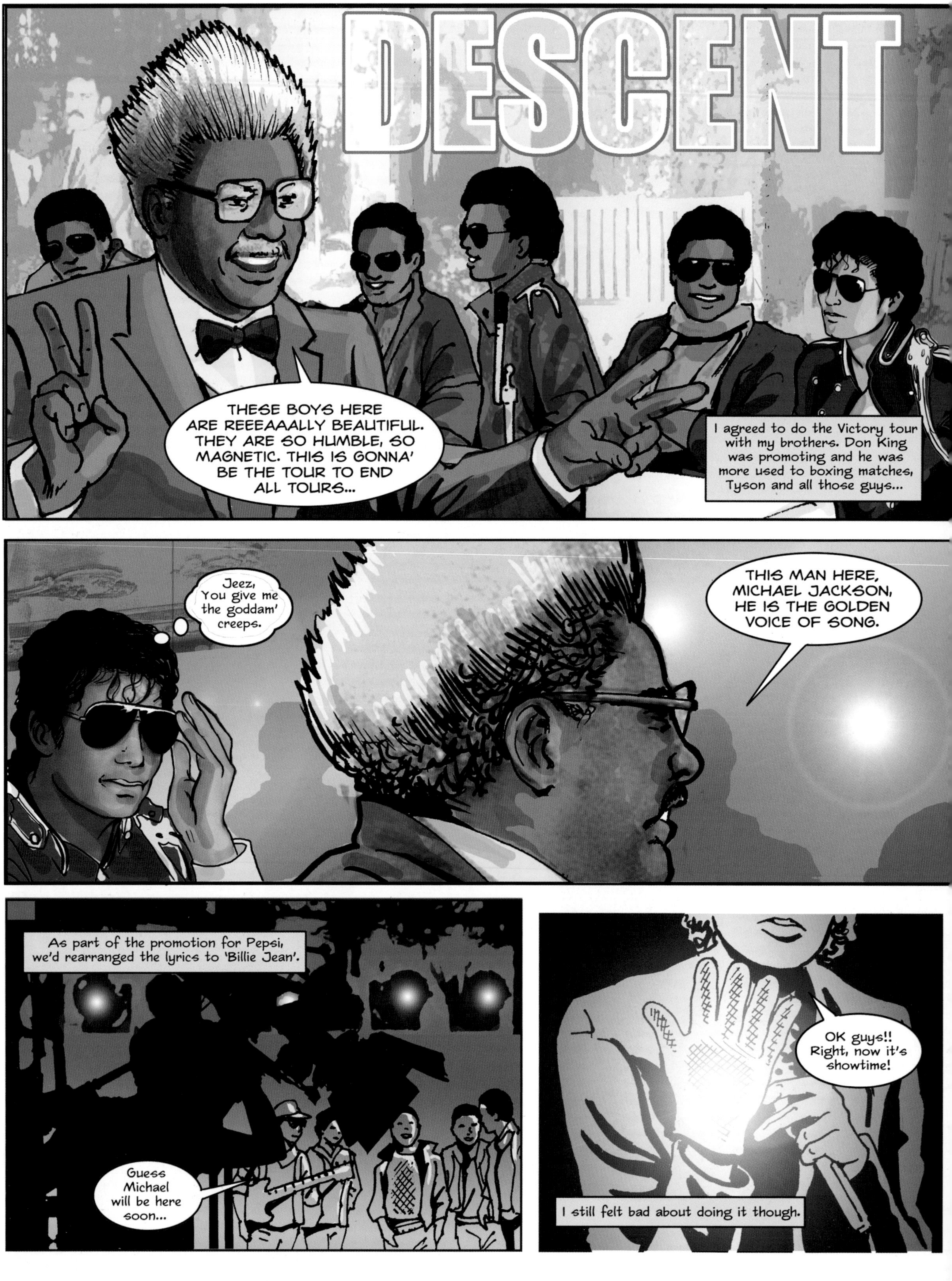
DESCENT
THESE BOYS HERE ARE REEEAAALLY BEAUTIFUL. THEY ARE SO HUMBLE, SO MAGNETIC. THIS IS GONNA' BE THE TOUR TO END ALL TOURS...
I agreed to do the Victory tour with my brothers. Don King was promoting and he was more used to boxing matches, Tyson and all those guys...
Jeez, You give me the goddam' creeps.
THIS MAN HERE, MICHAEL JACKSON, HE IS THE GOLDEN VOICE OF SONG.
As part of the promotion for Pepsi, we'd rearranged the lyrics to 'Billie Jean'.
Guess Michael will be here soon...
OK guys!! Right, now it's showtime!
I still felt bad about doing it though.

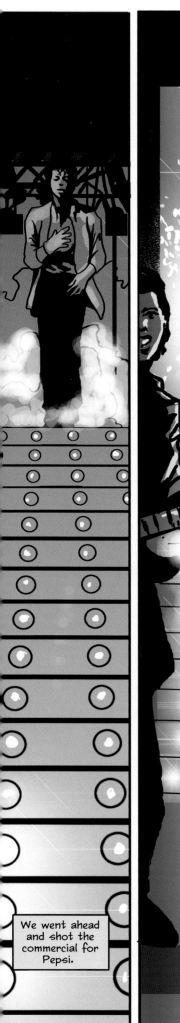

We went ahead and shot the commercial for Pepsi.

YOU'RE THE PEPSI GENERATION...

TITO! TITO!! WHAT IS HAPPENING MAN? MY HEAD IS ON FIRE!!

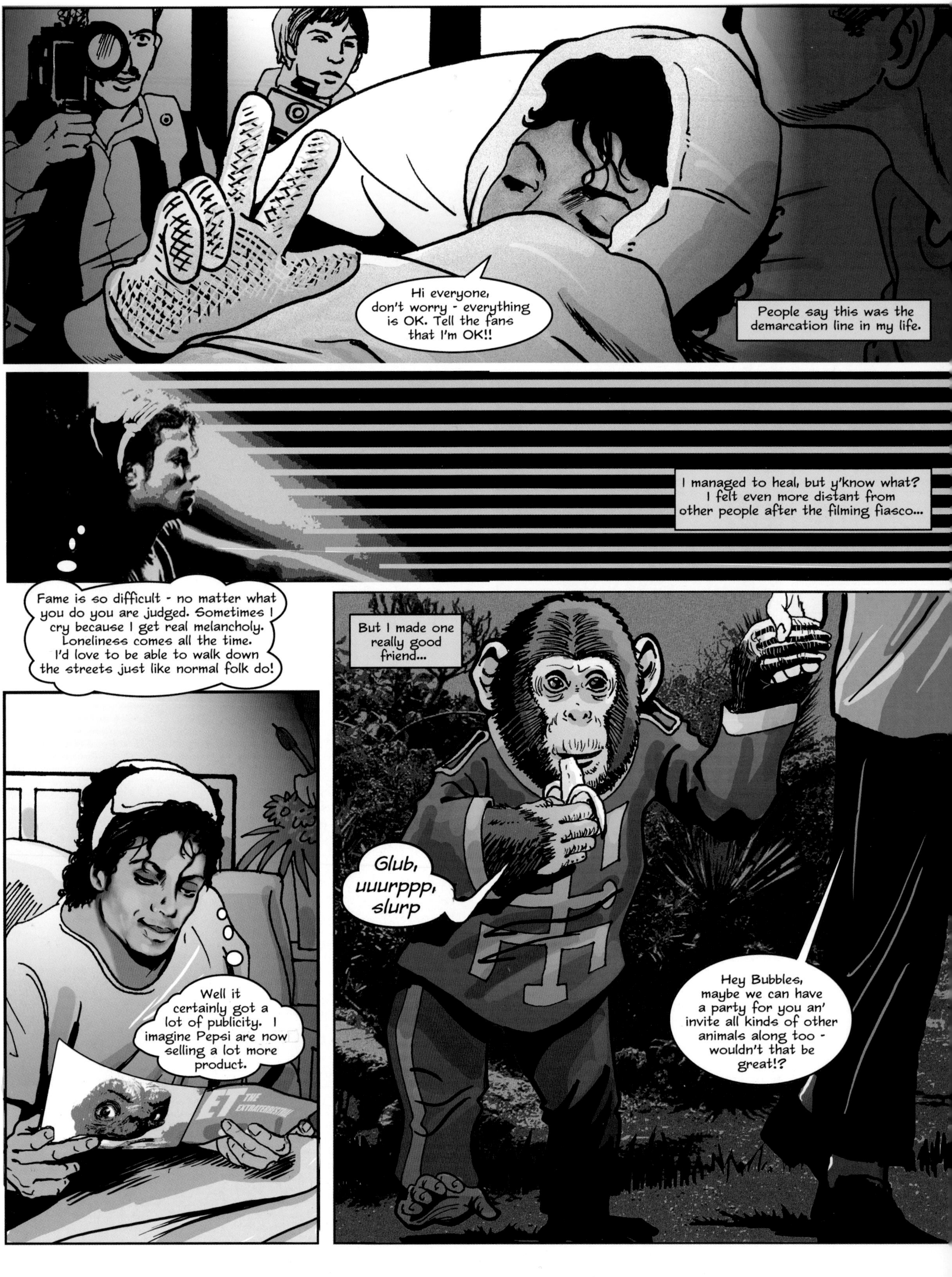

Hi everyone, don't worry - everything is OK. Tell the fans that I'm OK!!
People say this was the demarcation line in my life.
I managed to heal, but y'know what? I felt even more distant from other people after the filming fiasco...
Fame is so difficult - no matter what you do you are judged. Sometimes I cry because I get real melancholy. Loneliness comes all the time. I'd love to be able to walk down the streets just like normal folk do!
Well it certainly got a lot of publicity. I imagine Pepsi are now selling a lot more product.
ET THE EXTRATERRESTRIAL
But I made one really good friend...
Glub, uuurppp, slurp
Hey Bubbles, maybe we can have a party for you an' invite all kinds of other animals along too - wouldn't that be great!?

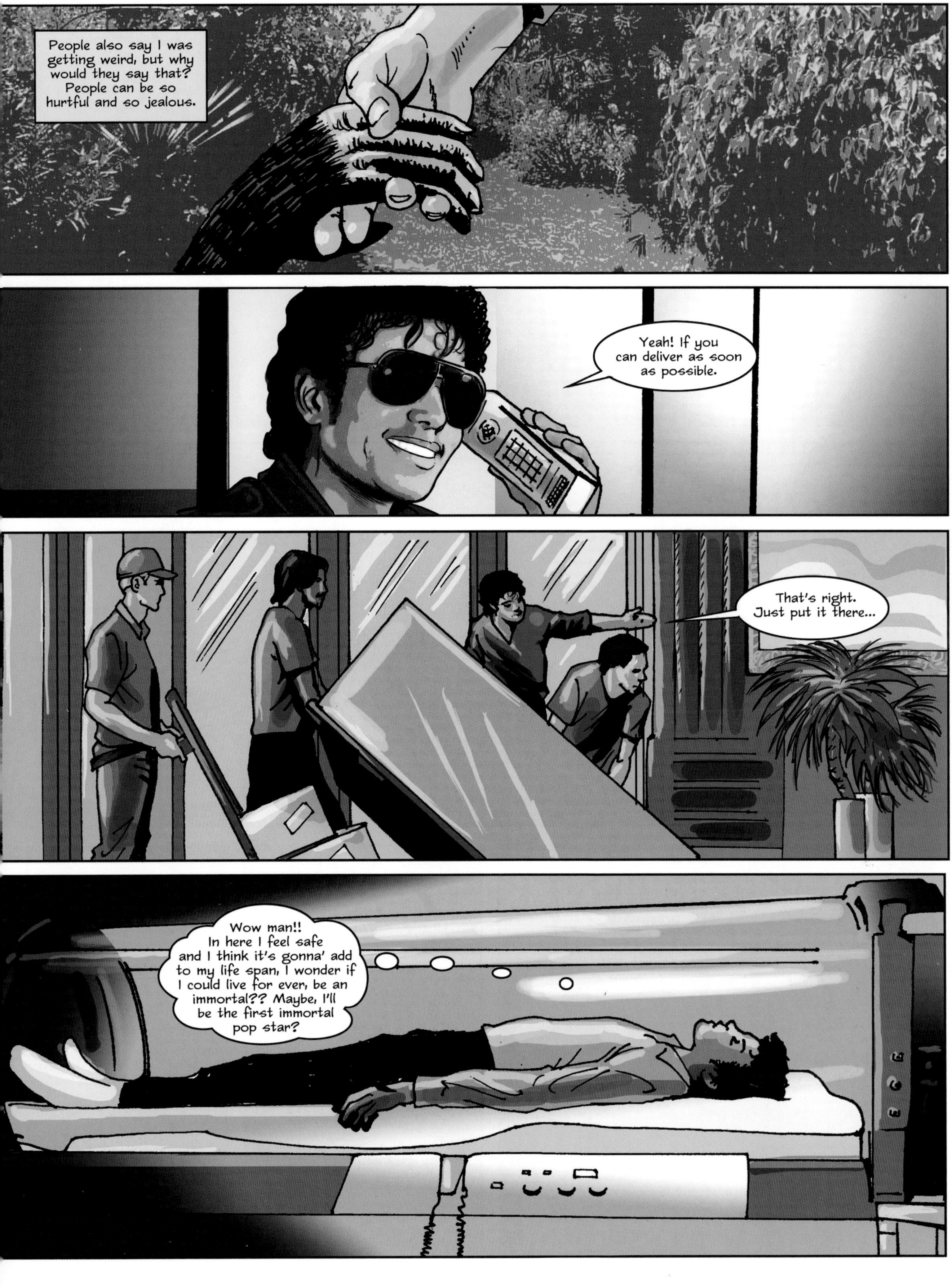

People also say I was getting weird, but why would they say that? People can be so hurtful and so jealous.
Yeah! If you can deliver as soon as possible.
That's right. Just put it there...
Wow man!! In here I feel safe and I think it's gonna' add to my life span, I wonder if I could live for ever, be an immortal?? Maybe, I'll be the first immortal pop star?

Was I joking or not - I guess nobody found out.
This thing with the oxygen chamber. Michael thinks he's going to live to be 150 years old! I think it's damn dangerous!
While the press are thinking about that, I'm working on another money maker...
JACKSON BUYS BEATLES CATALOGUE
They're mine now... I got 'em!! I got 'em!!
I did it. I outbid Paul McCartney and Yoko Ono. I own The Beatles catalogue!!!
Something else I wanted to buy was a little stranger... Joseph Merrick's remains, who was also known as The Elephant Man, are housed at The London College Hospital in London city.
The world press will go nuts if they think I want to buy The Elephant Man's remains...
Well Frank, if they want more, let's offer them more for his remains - go ahead!
I thought it was the perfect publicity stunt, particularly after the oxygen chamber.
LONDON COLLEGE HOSPITAL.
Well, we at the hospital have read it in the papers, but we cannot confirm that Mr Jackson has indeed actually made an offer at this time.
Mr Jackson is now prepared to offer you a million dollars for the bones of Mr Merrick.
Yes!! That's correct, a million dollars!

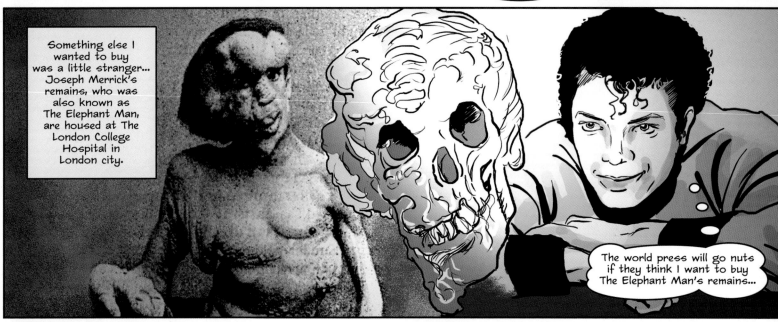

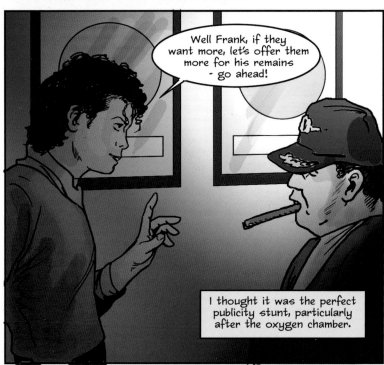

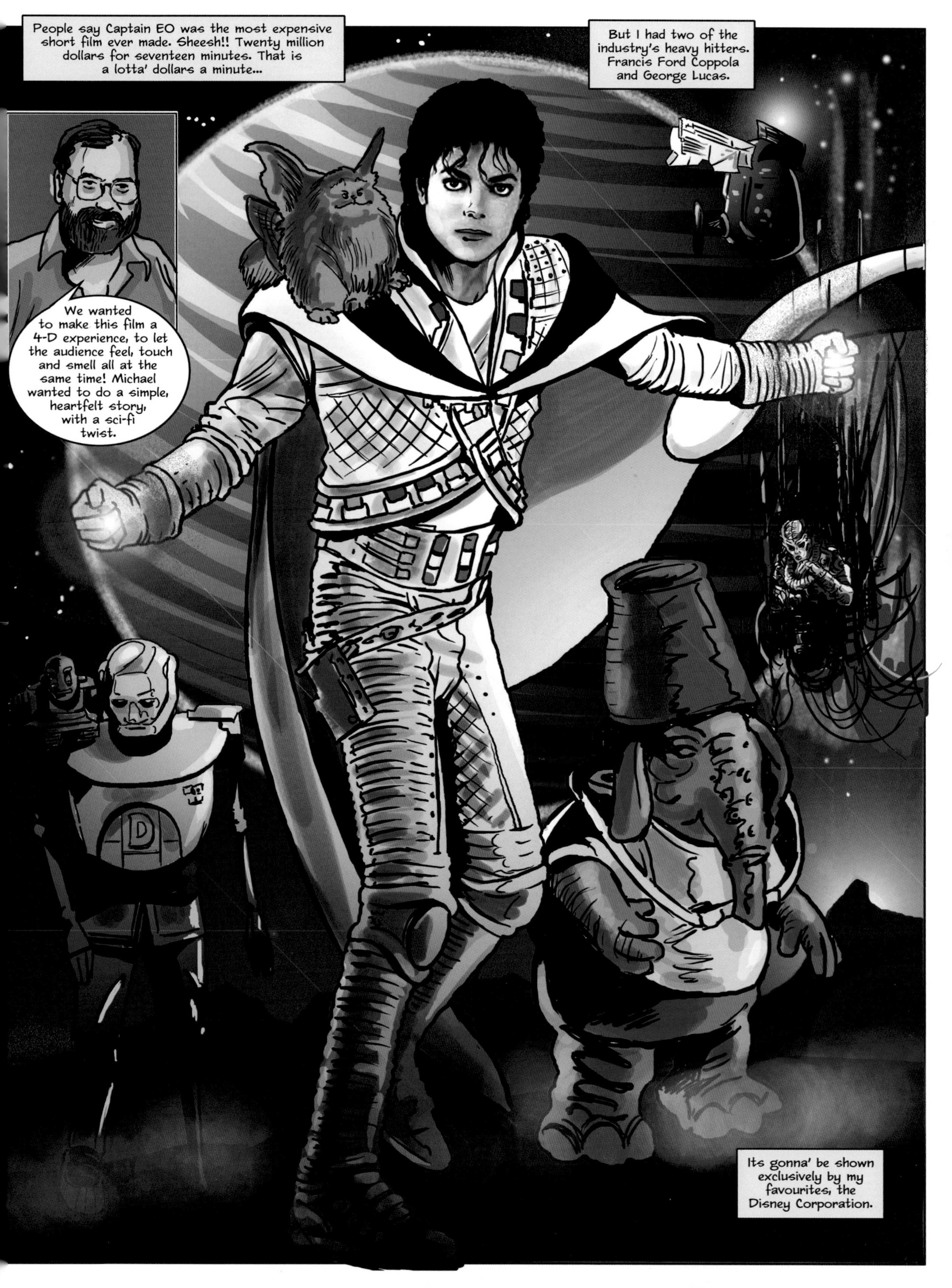
People say Captain EO was the most expensive short film ever made. Sheesh!! Twenty million dollars for seventeen minutes. That is a lotta' dollars a minute...
But I had two of the industry's heavy hitters. Francis Ford Coppola and George Lucas.
We wanted to make this film a 4-D experience, to let the audience feel, touch and smell all at the same time! Michael wanted to do a simple, heartfelt story, with a sci-fi twist.
D
Its gonna' be shown exclusively by my favourites, the Disney Corporation.

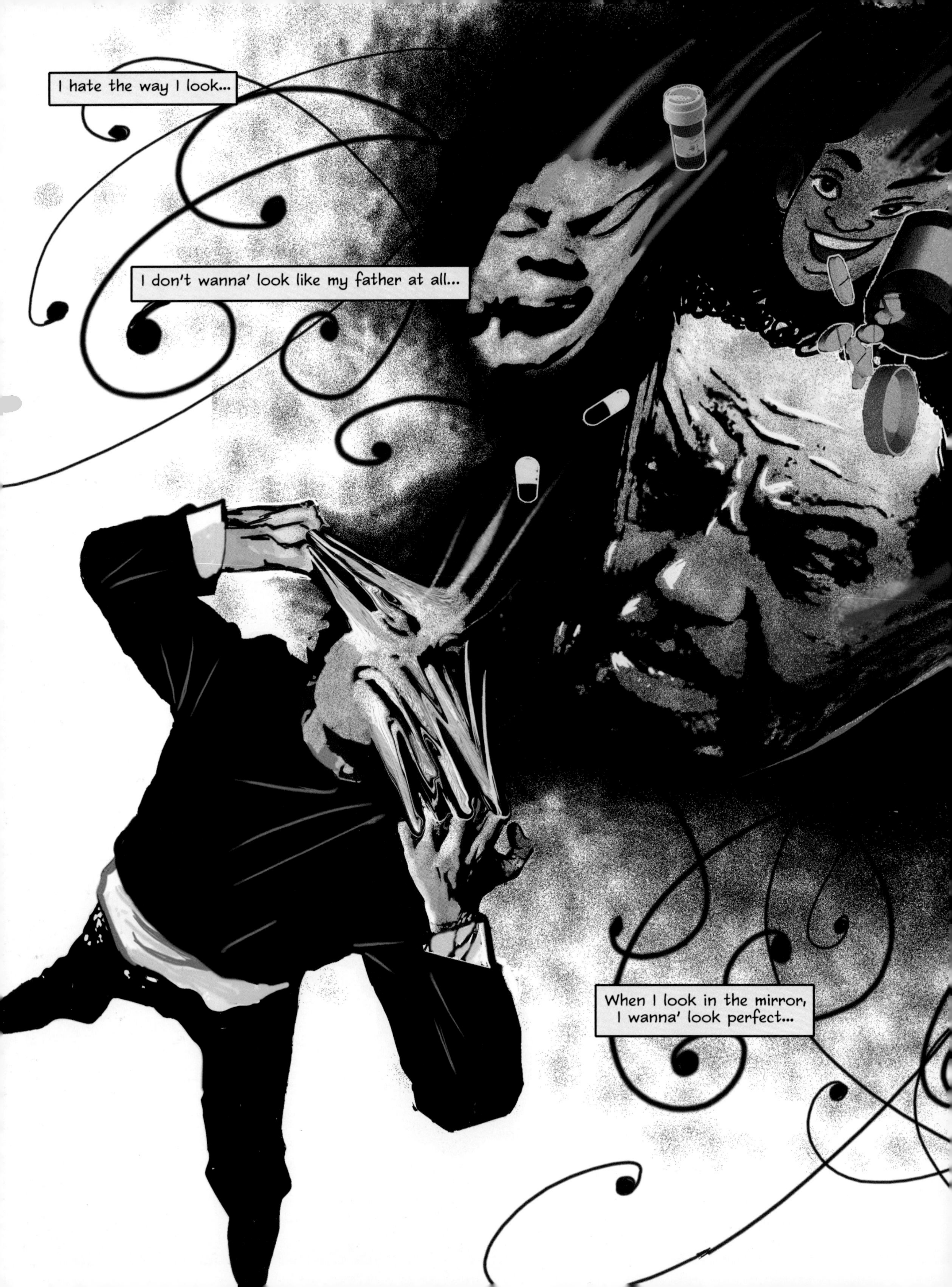
I hate the way I look...
I don't wanna' look like my father at all...
When I look in the mirror, I wanna' look perfect...

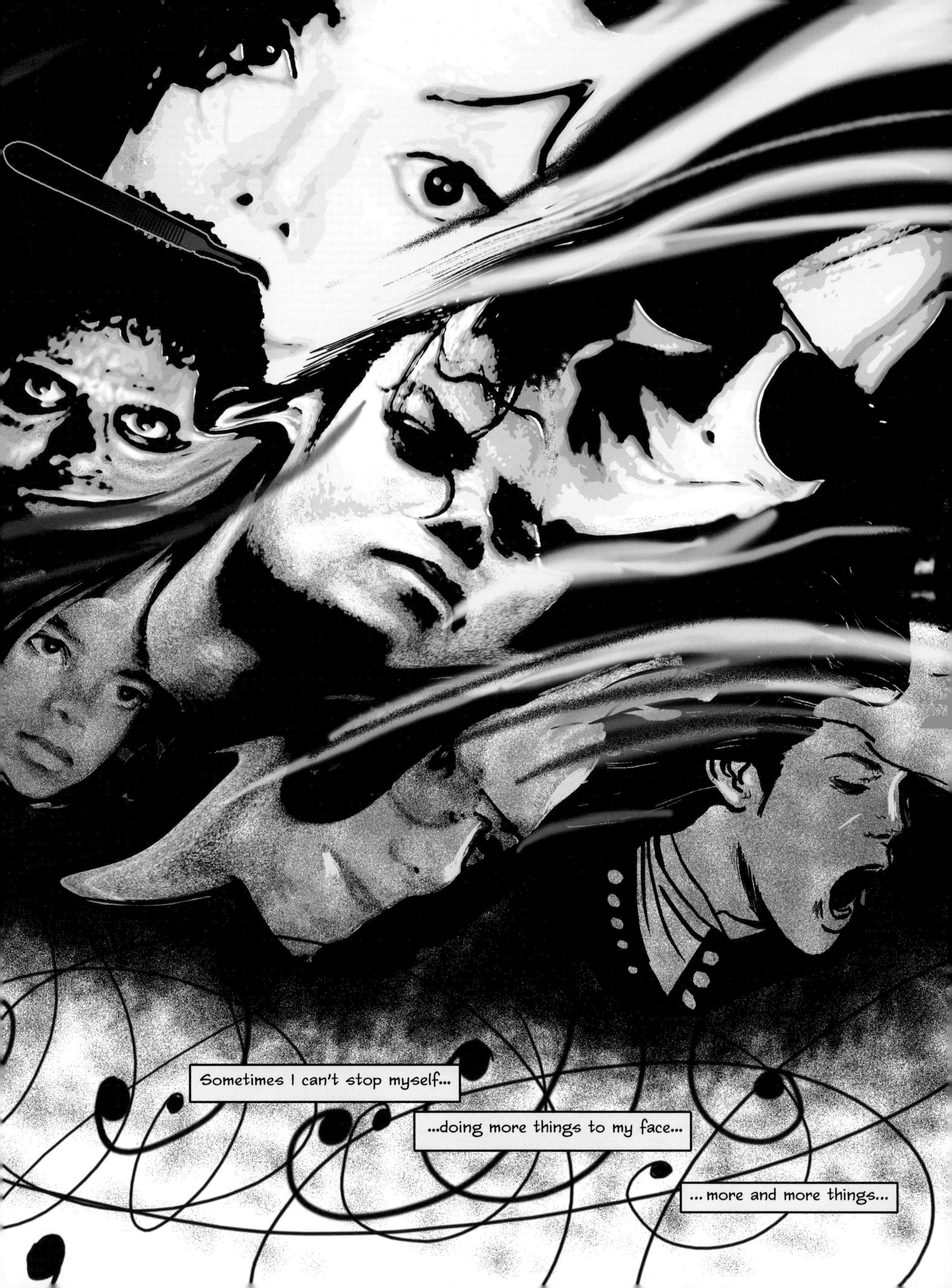
Sometimes I can't stop myself...
...doing more things to my face...
... more and more things...

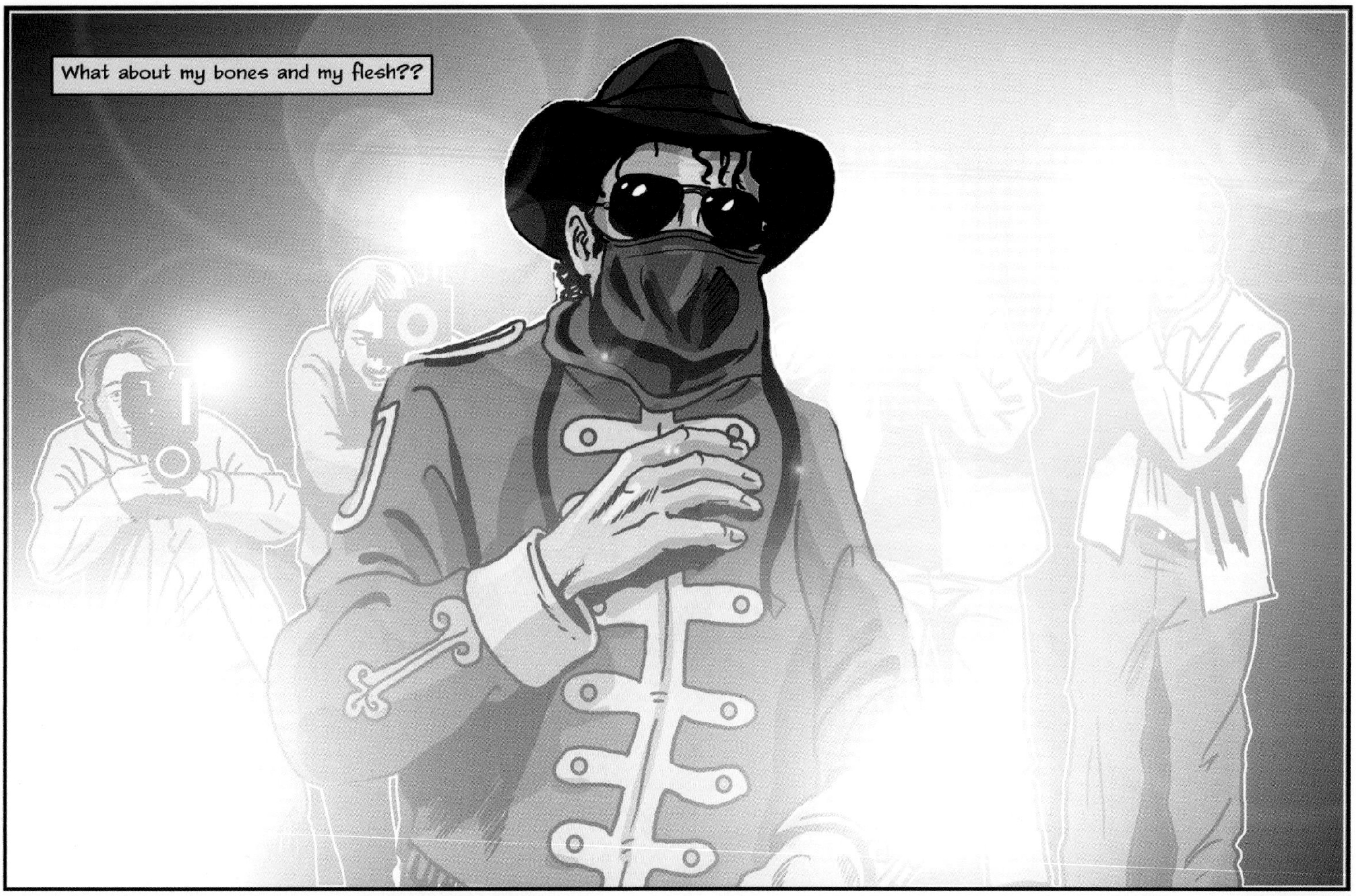
What about my bones and my flesh??

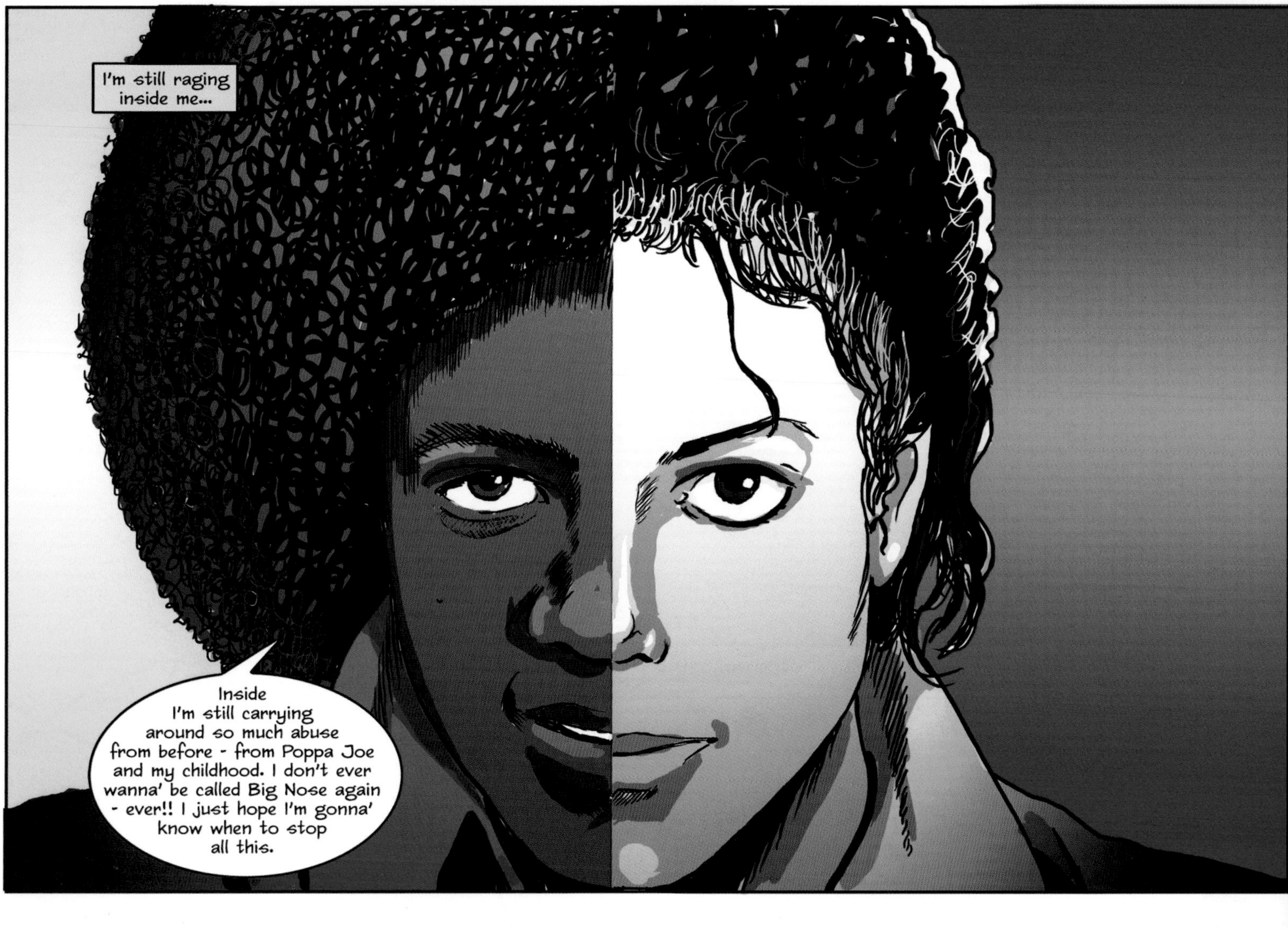
I'm still raging inside me...
Inside I'm still carrying around so much abuse from before - from Poppa Joe and my childhood. I don't ever wanna' be called Big Nose again - ever!! I just hope I'm gonna' know when to stop all this.

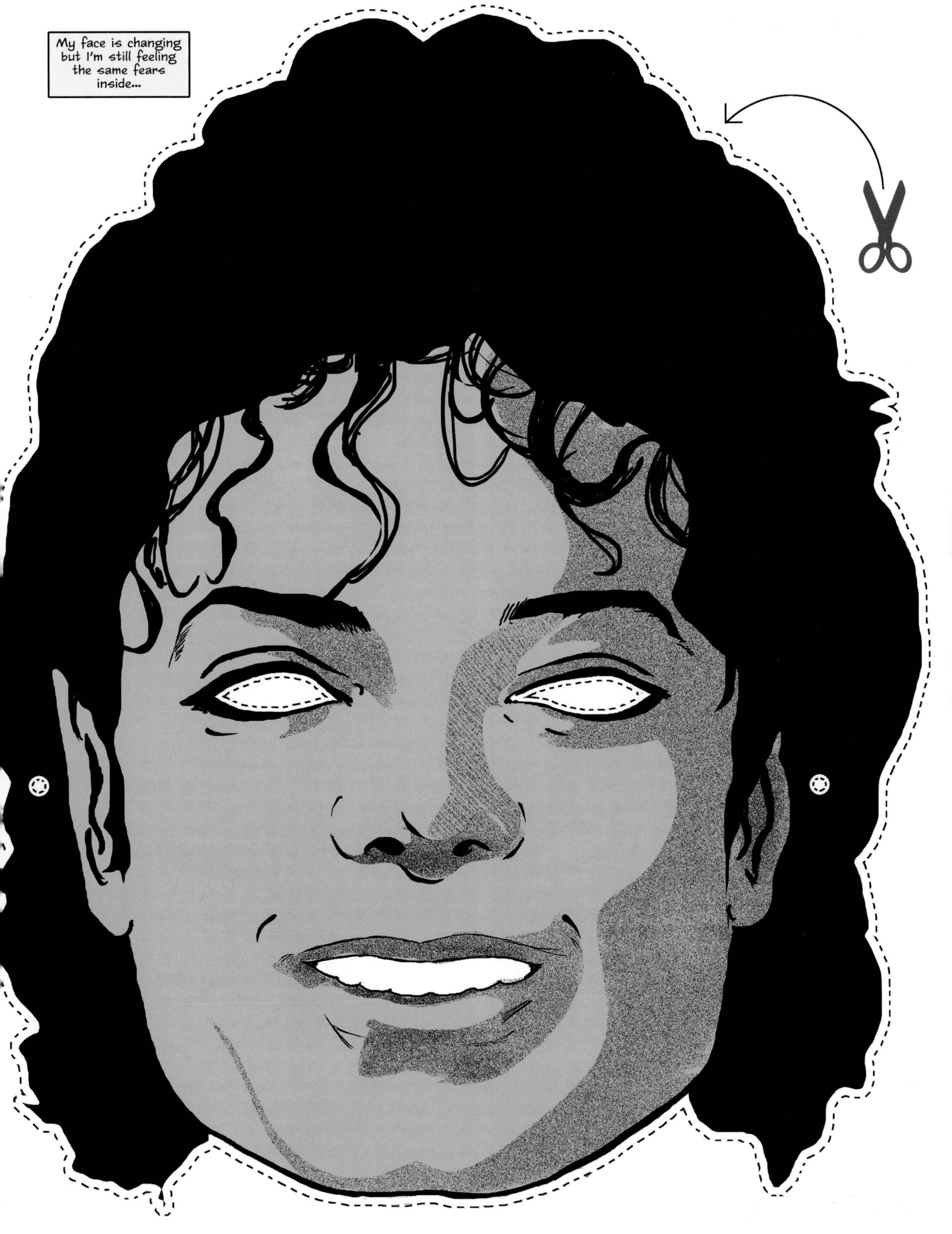
My face is changing but I'm still feeling the same fears inside...

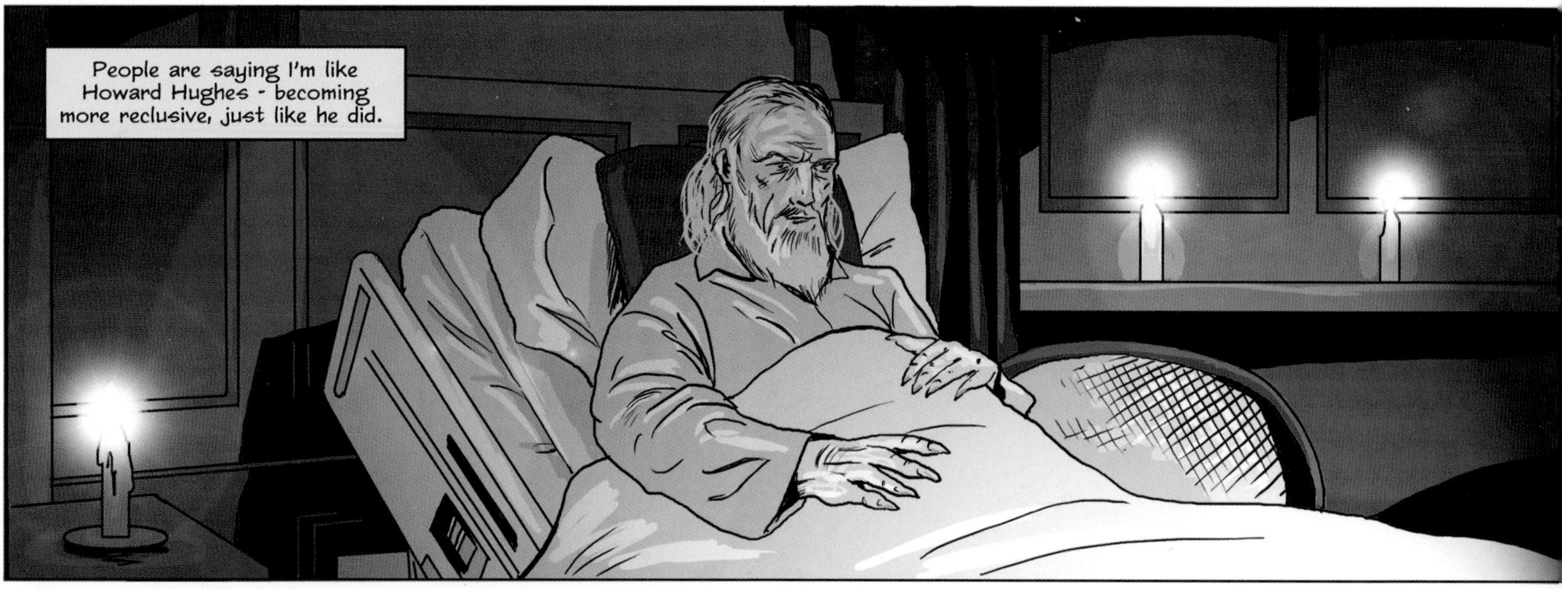
People are saying I'm like Howard Hughes - becoming more reclusive, just like he did.

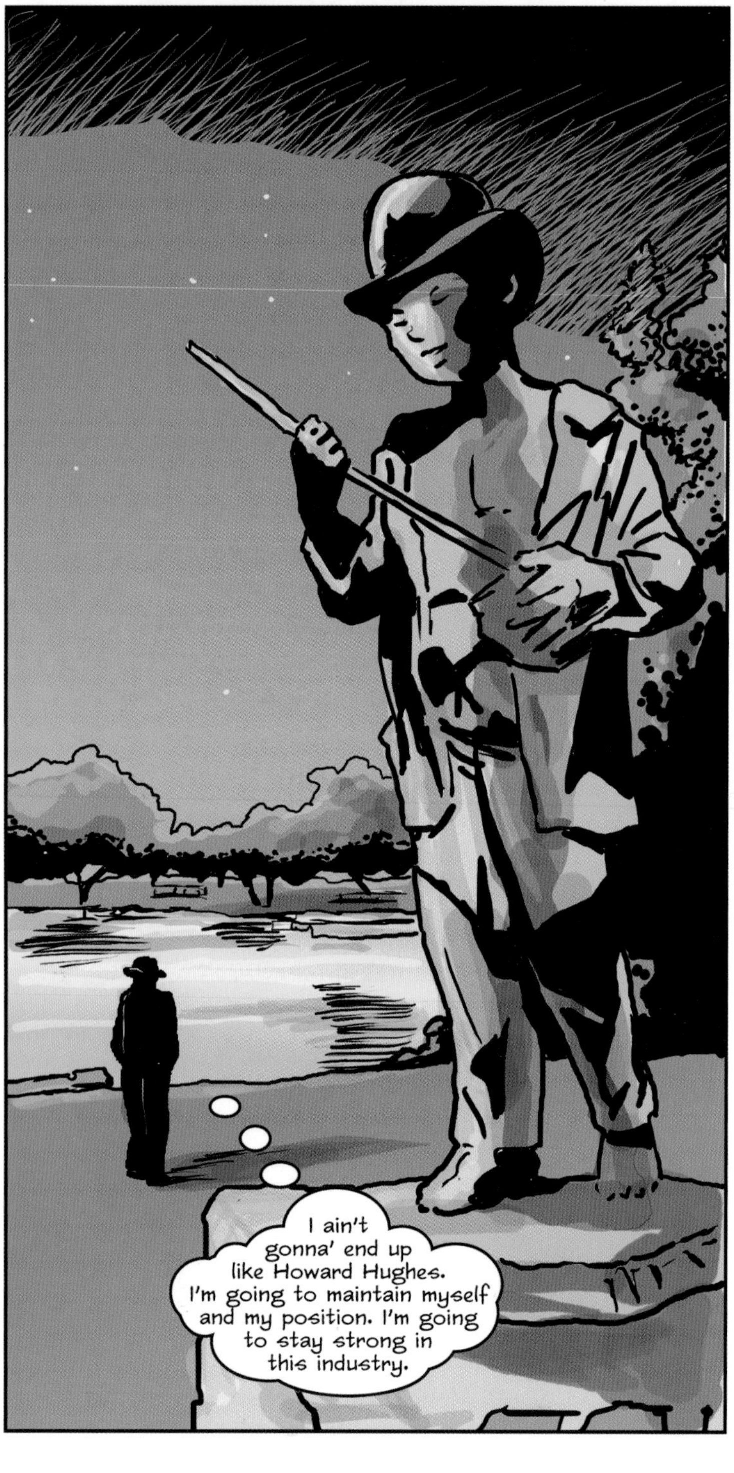
I ain't gonna' end up like Howard Hughes. I'm going to maintain myself and my position. I'm going to stay strong in this industry.

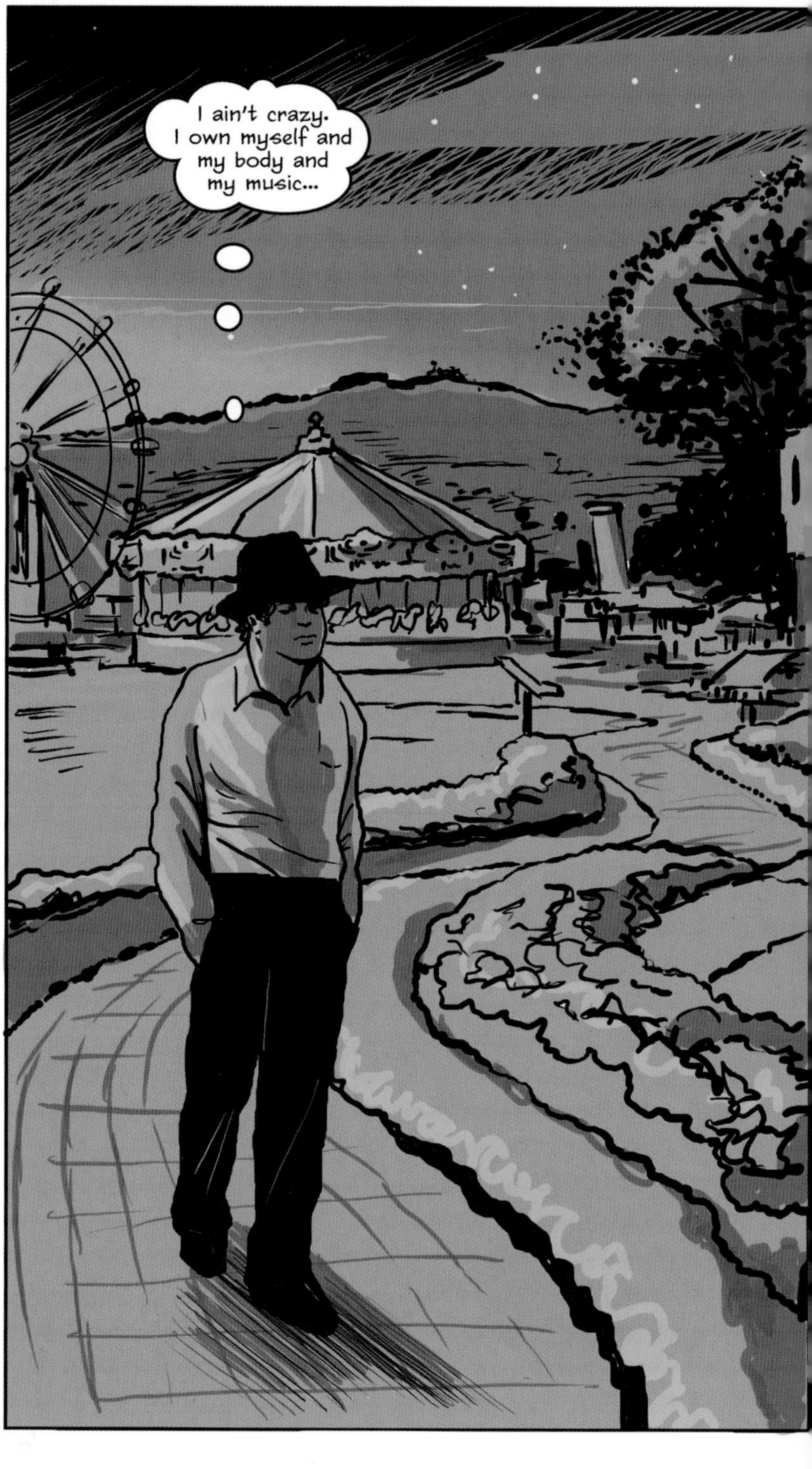
I ain't crazy. I own myself and my body and my music...

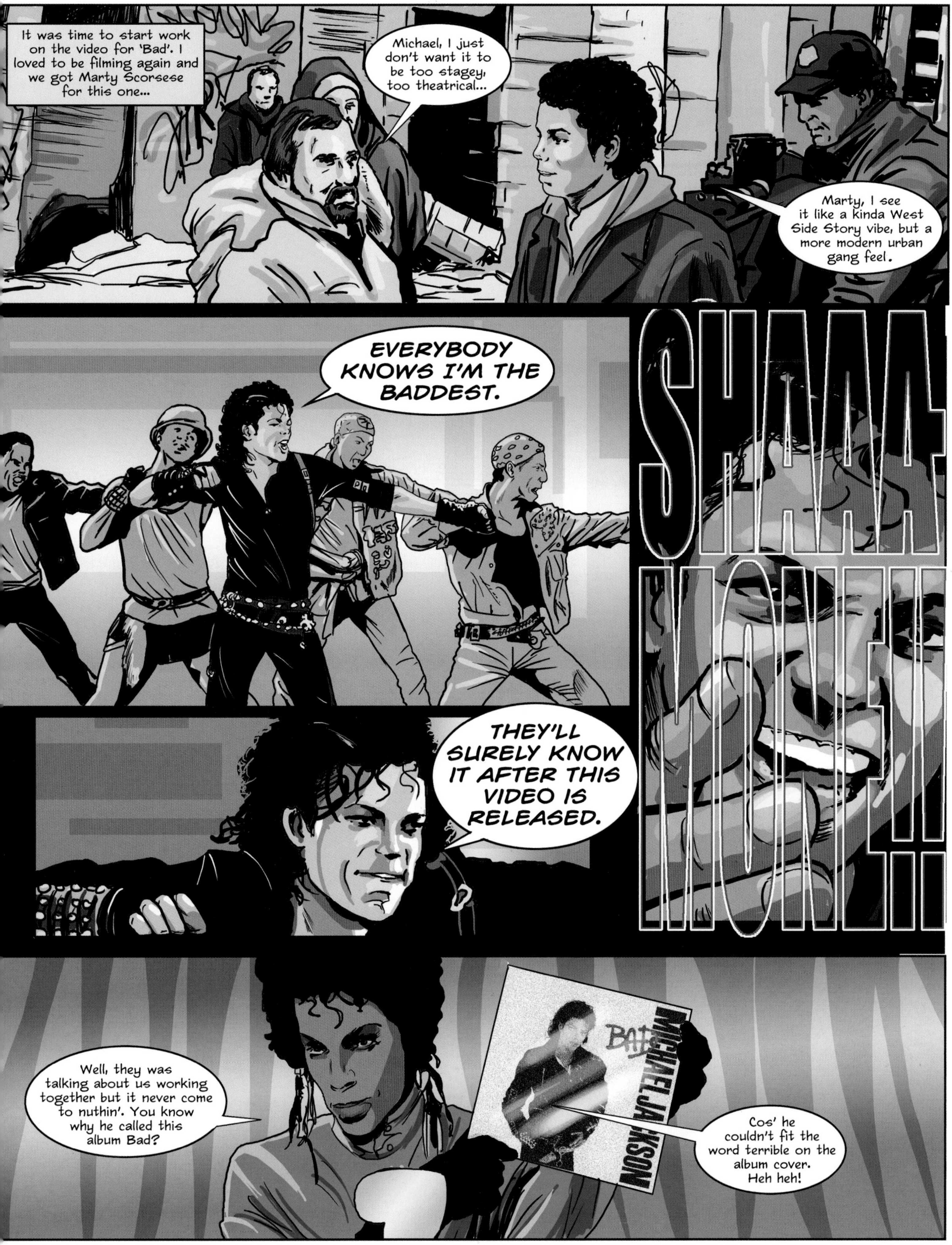
It was time to start work on the video for 'Bad'. I loved to be filming again and we got Marty Scorsese for this one...
Michael, I just don't want it to be too stagey, too theatrical...
Marty, I see it like a kinda West Side Story vibe, but a more modern urban gang feel.
EVERYBODY KNOWS I'M THE BADDEST.
THEY'LL SURELY KNOW IT AFTER THIS VIDEO IS RELEASED.
SHAAA
MONE!!!
Well, they was talking about us working together but it never come to nuthin'. You know why he called this album Bad?
Cos' he couldn't fit the word terrible on the album cover. Heh heh!

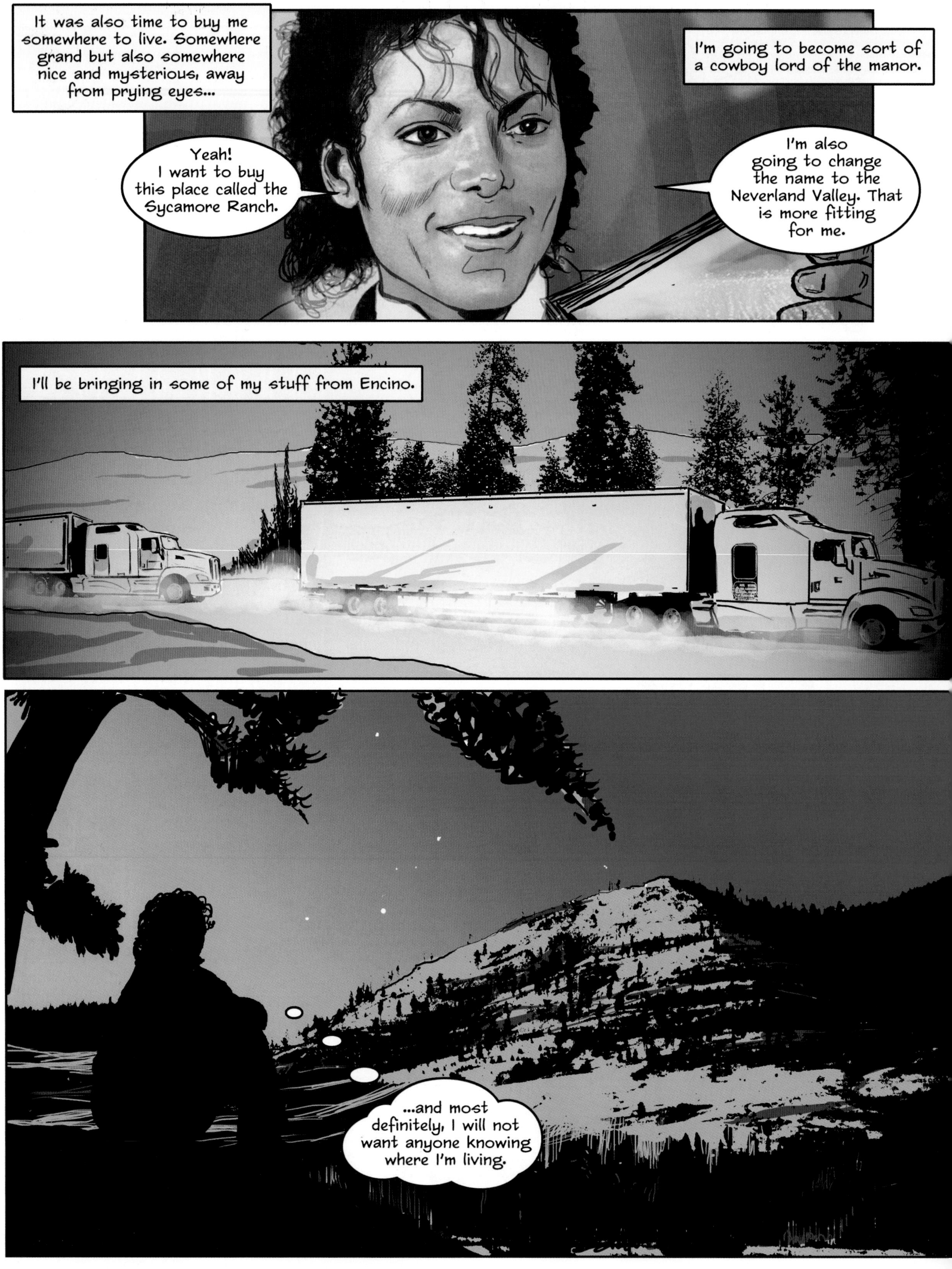
It was also time to buy me somewhere to live. Somewhere grand but also somewhere nice and mysterious, away from prying eyes...
Yeah! I want to buy this place called the Sycamore Ranch.
I'm going to become sort of a cowboy lord of the manor.
I'm also going to change the name to the Neverland Valley. That is more fitting for me.
I'll be bringing in some of my stuff from Encino.
...and most definitely, I will not want anyone knowing where I'm living.

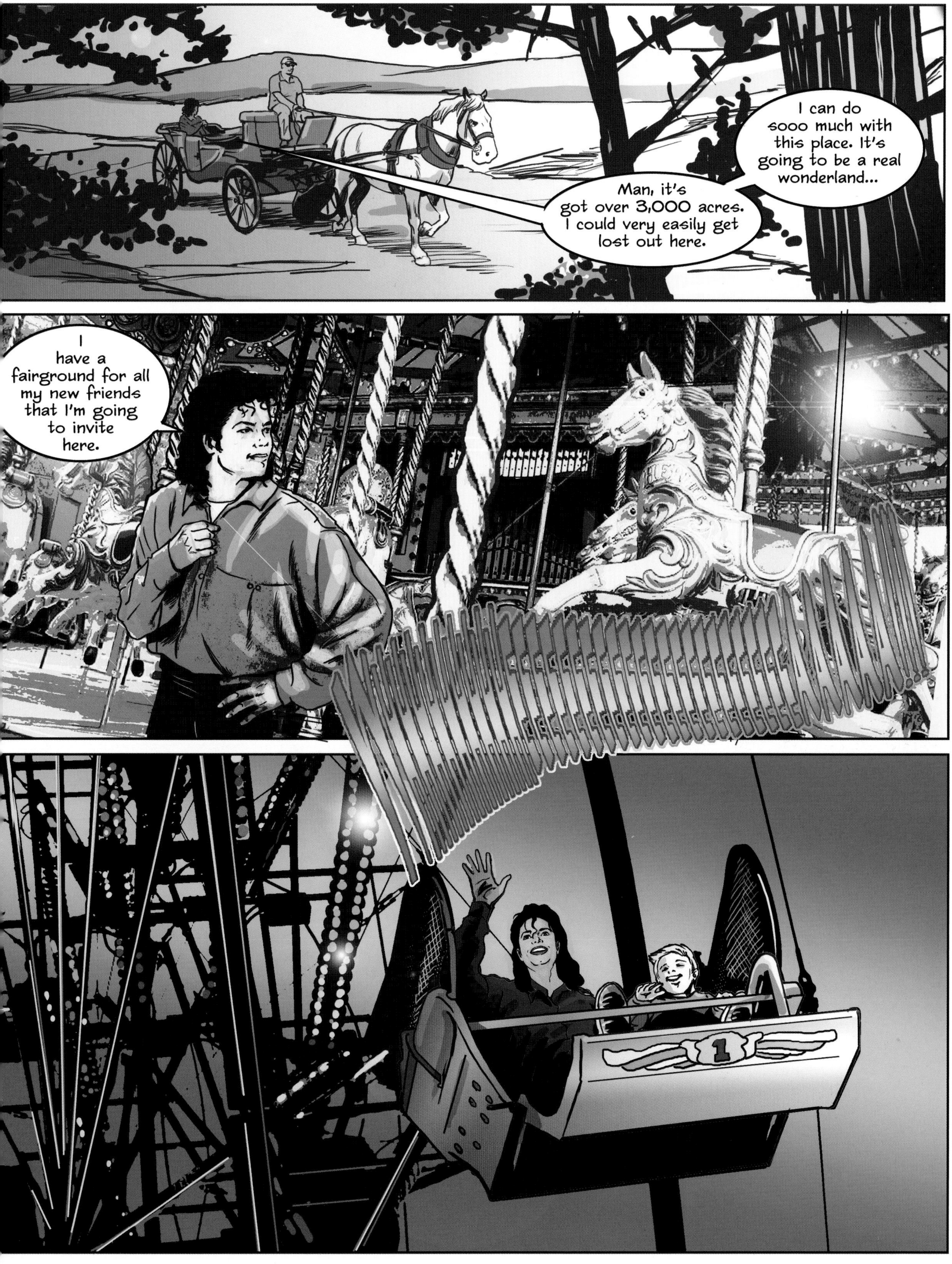
Man, it's got over 3,000 acres. I could very easily get lost out here.
I can do sooo much with this place. It's going to be a real wonderland...
I have a fairground for all my new friends that I'm going to invite here.

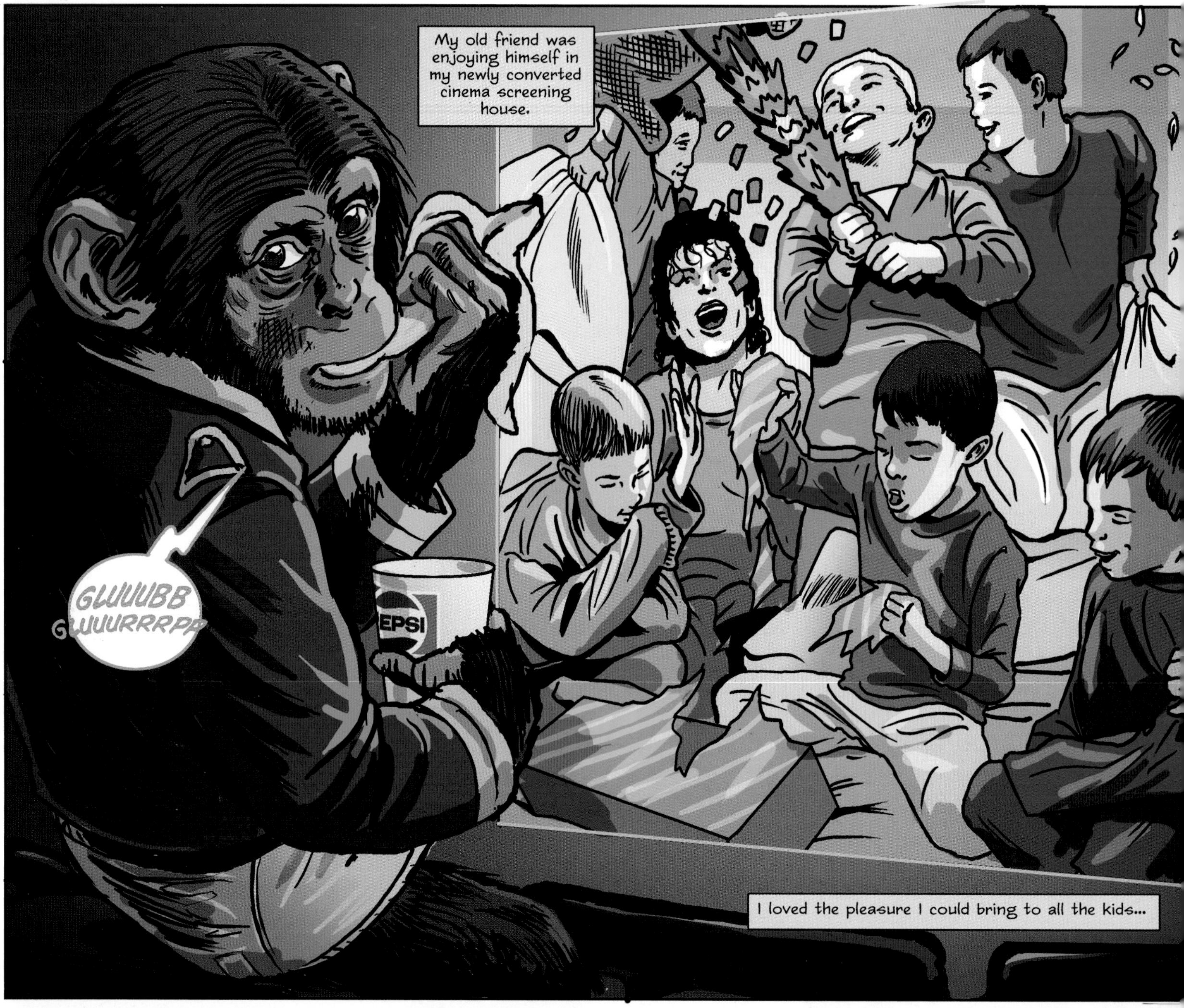
My old friend was enjoying himself in my newly converted cinema screening house.
GLUUUBB GLUUURRRPP
PEPSI
I loved the pleasure I could bring to all the kids...

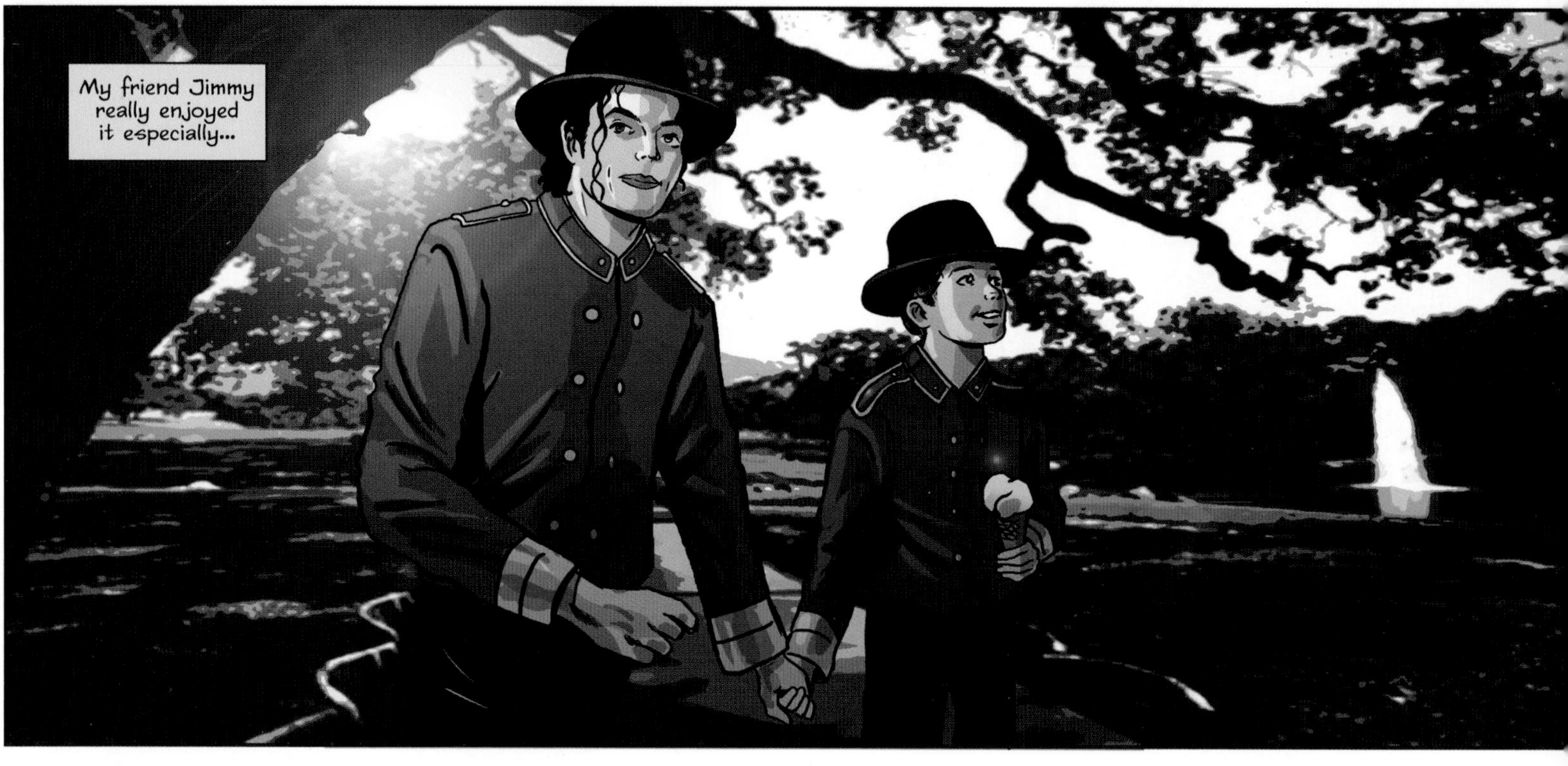
My friend Jimmy really enjoyed it especially...

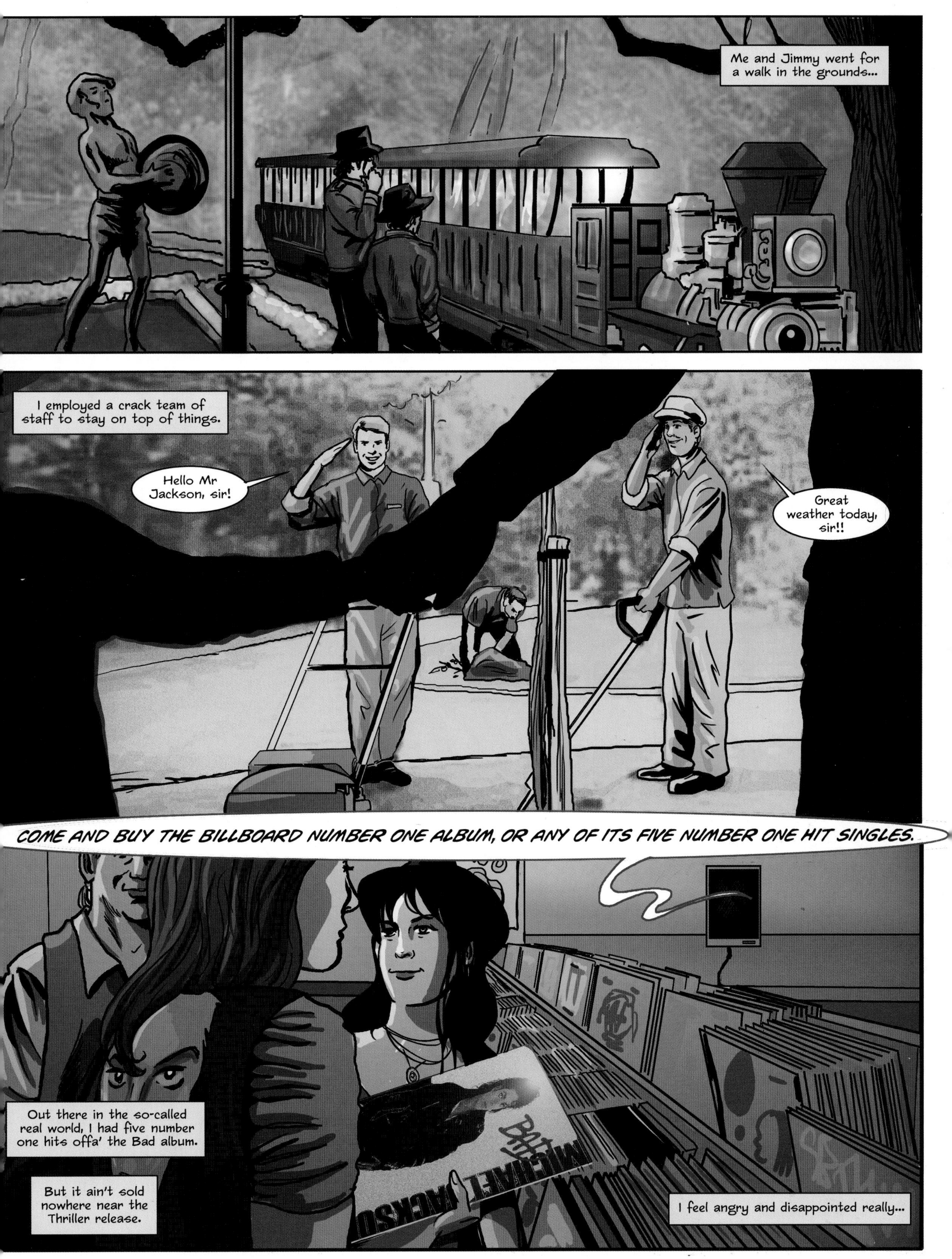
Me and Jimmy went for a walk in the grounds...
I employed a crack team of staff to stay on top of things.
Hello Mr Jackson, sir!
Great weather today, sir!!
COME AND BUY THE BILLBOARD NUMBER ONE ALBUM, OR ANY OF ITS FIVE NUMBER ONE HIT SINGLES.
Out there in the so-called real world, I had five number one hits offa' the Bad album.
But it ain't sold nowhere near the Thriller release.
I feel angry and disappointed really...

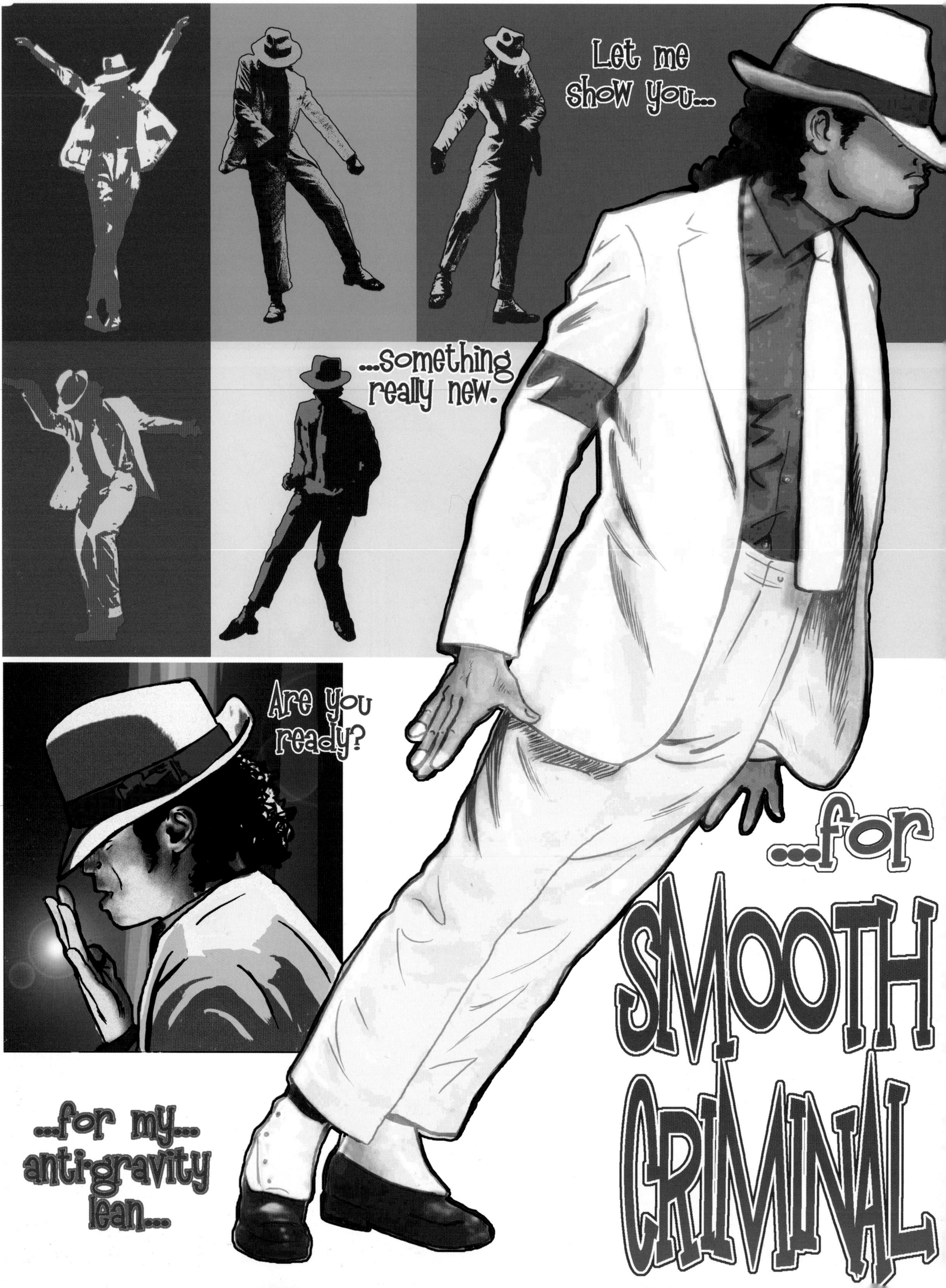
Let me show you...
...something really new.
Are you ready?
...for my... anti-gravity lean...
...for SMOOTH CRIMINAL

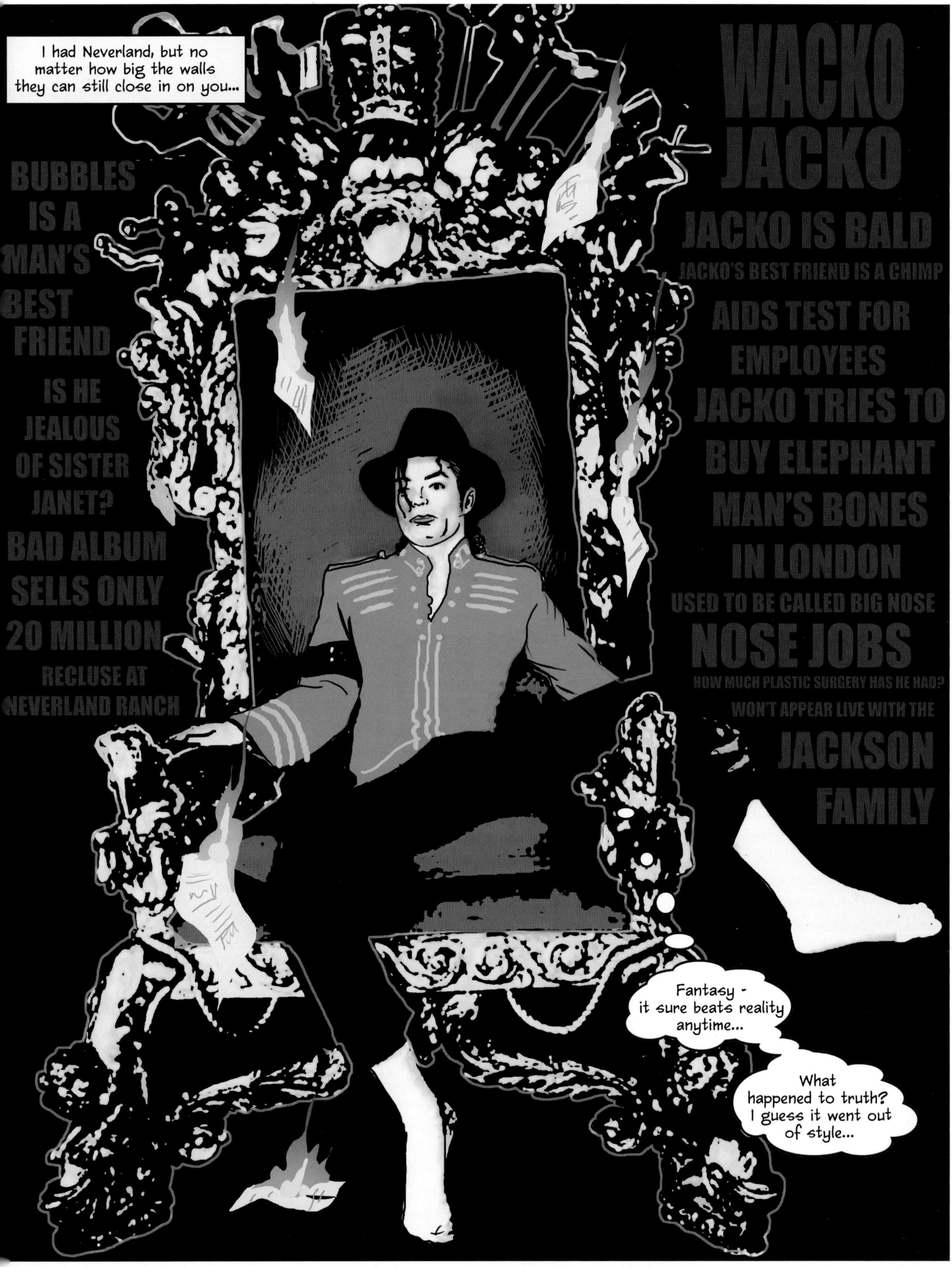

I had Neverland, but no matter how big the walls they can still close in on you...
WACKO JACKO
BUBBLES IS A MAN'S BEST FRIEND
JACKO IS BALD
JACKO'S BEST FRIEND IS A CHIMP
AIDS TEST FOR EMPLOYEES
IS HE JEALOUS OF SISTER JANET?
JACKO TRIES TO BUY ELEPHANT MAN'S BONES IN LONDON
BAD ALBUM SELLS ONLY 20 MILLION
USED TO BE CALLED BIG NOSE
NOSE JOBS
RECLUSE AT NEVERLAND RANCH
HOW MUCH PLASTIC SURGERY HAS HE HAD?
WON'T APPEAR LIVE WITH THE JACKSON FAMILY
Fantasy - it sure beats reality anytime...
What happened to truth? I guess it went out of style...

Well, I guess I'm about ready... Is Michael ready yet??

I went ahead with a massive interview with Oprah Winfrey on February 10, 1993. It was going to reach 90 million people.

I believe I really missed out on growing up, It was all work, work and more work.

I remember going to the recording studio, and there was a park across the street, and I'd see all the children playing and I would cry.

It would make me sad that I would have to go to work instead.

What about the skin lightening Michael??

Well, yes! I have a skin condition called vitiligo, where my skin gets blotchy. It is something I cannot help.

When people make up stories that I don't want to be who I am, it hurts me. It's a problem for me. I can't control it.

But what about all the millions of people who sit in the sun to become darker, to try and become other than what they are. Nobody says nothing about that.

How about your father Joe, Michael, your childhood with him?

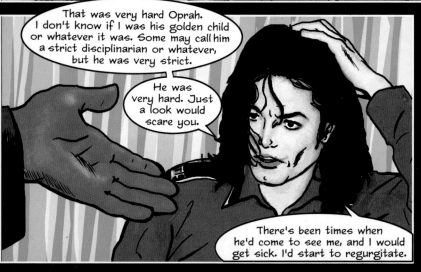

That was very hard Oprah. I don't know if I was his golden child or whatever it was. Some may call him a strict disciplinarian or whatever, but he was very strict.

He was very hard. Just a look would scare you.

There's been times when he'd come to see me, and I would get sick. I'd start to regurgitate.

I gave Oprah a night time tour too...

Let me show you around with the crew

This is a really good night out here.

The stars just go on for ever and ever in the universe.

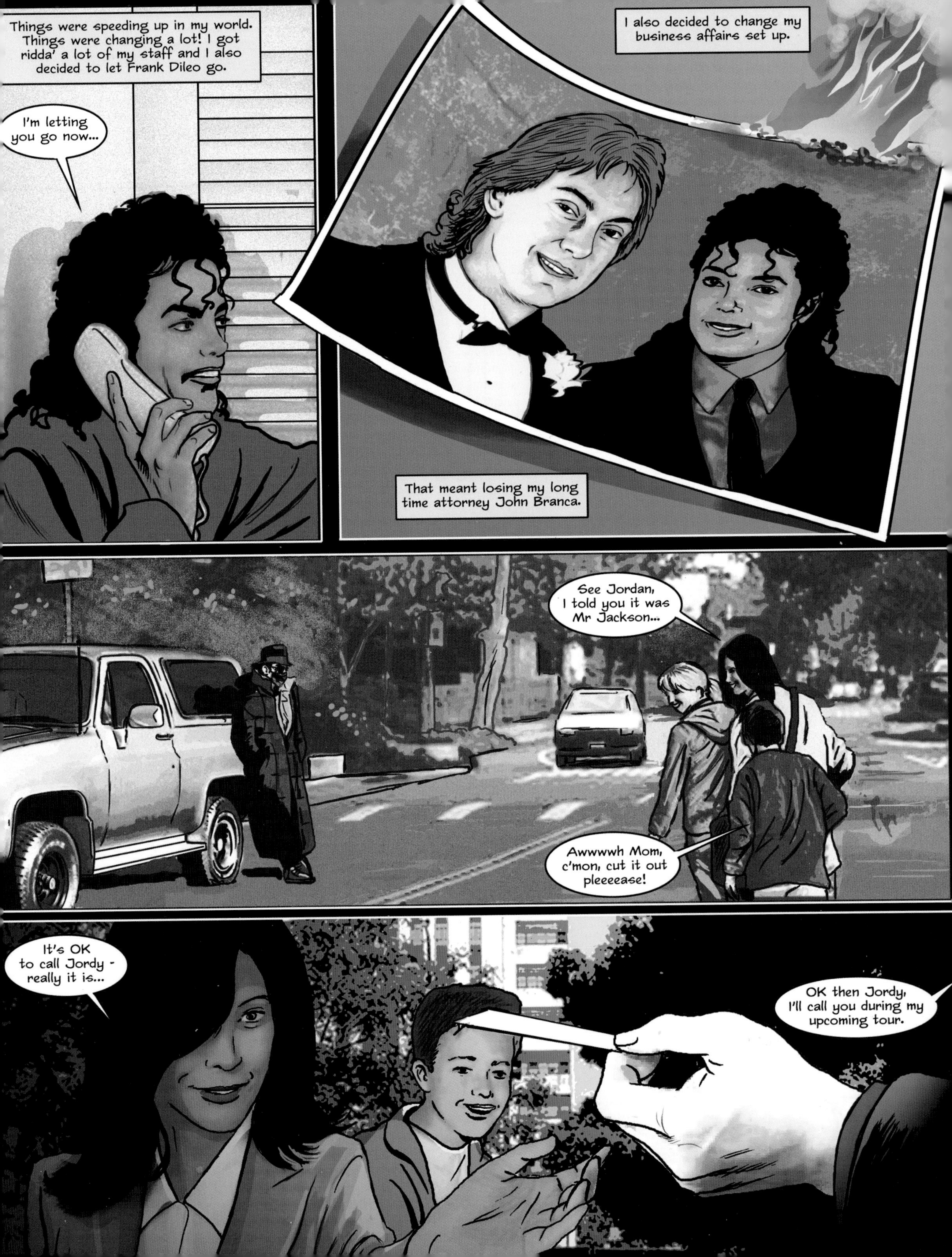
Things were speeding up in my world. Things were changing a lot! I got ridda' a lot of my staff and I also decided to let Frank Dileo go.
I'm letting you go now...
I also decided to change my business affairs set up.
That meant losing my long time attorney John Branca.
See Jordan, I told you it was Mr Jackson...
Awwwwh Mom, c'mon, cut it out pleeeease!
It's OK to call Jordy - really it is...
OK then Jordy, I'll call you during my upcoming tour.

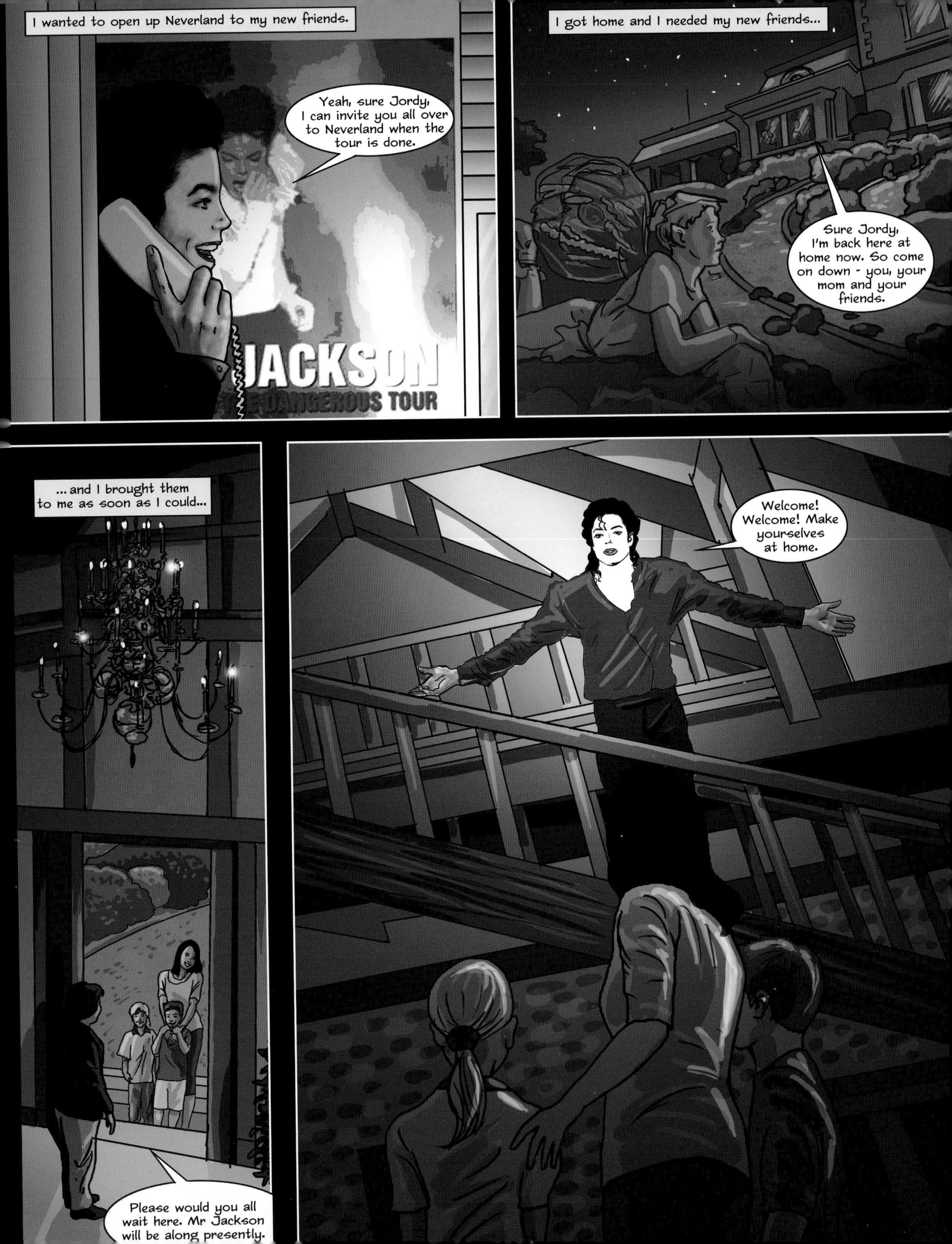

I wanted to open up Neverland to my new friends.
Yeah, sure Jordy, I can invite you all over to Neverland when the tour is done.
JACKSON
DANGEROUS TOUR
I got home and I needed my new friends...
Sure Jordy, I'm back here at home now. So come on down - you, your mom and your friends.
...and I brought them to me as soon as I could...
Please would you all wait here. Mr Jackson will be along presently.
Welcome! Welcome! Make yourselves at home.

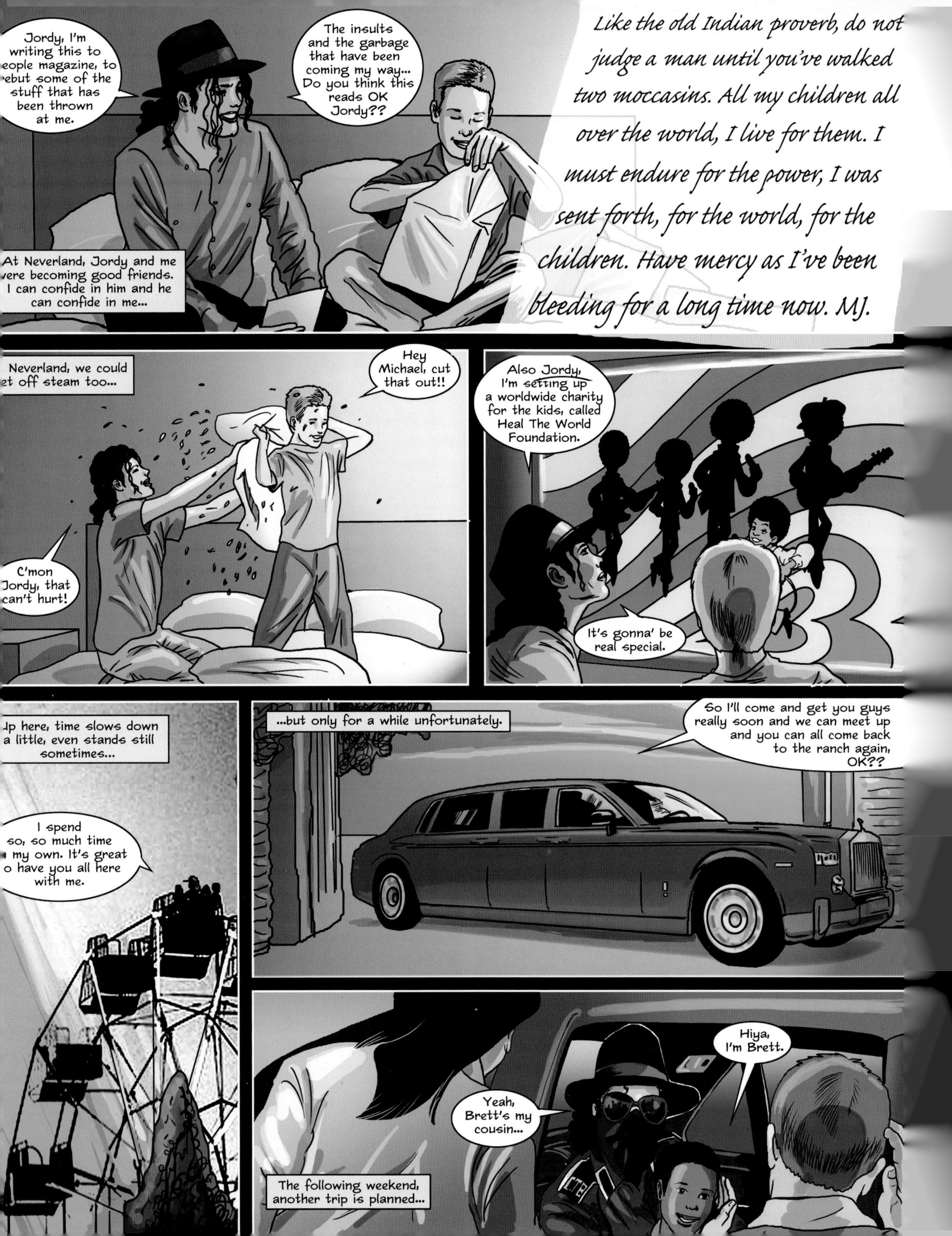
Jordy, I'm writing this to eople magazine, to ebut some of the stuff that has been thrown at me.
The insults and the garbage that have been coming my way... Do you think this reads OK Jordy??
At Neverland, Jordy and me vere becoming good friends. I can confide in him and he can confide in me...
Like the old Indian proverb, do not judge a man until you've walked two moccasins. All my children all over the world, I live for them. I must endure for the power, I was sent forth, for the world, for the children. Have mercy as I've been bleeding for a long time now. MJ.
Neverland, we could et off steam too...
Hey Michael, cut that out!!
C'mon Jordy, that can't hurt!
Also Jordy, I'm setting up a worldwide charity for the kids, called Heal The World Foundation.
It's gonna' be real special.
Jp here, time slows down a little, even stands still sometimes...
I spend so, so much time my own. It's great o have you all here with me.
...but only for a while unfortunately.
So I'll come and get you guys really soon and we can meet up and you can all come back to the ranch again, OK??
Hiya, I'm Brett.
Yeah, Brett's my cousin...
The following weekend, another trip is planned...

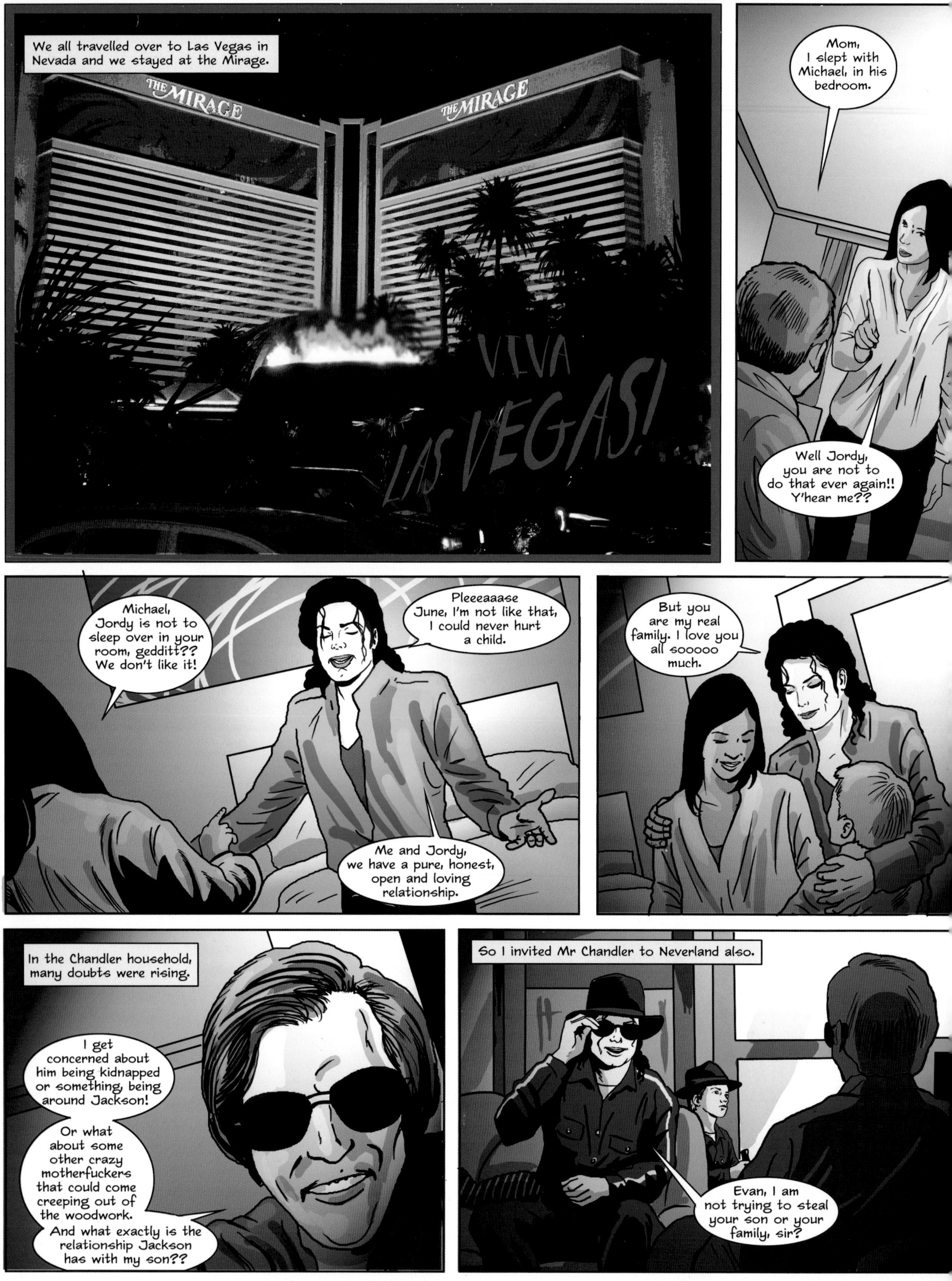

We all travelled over to Las Vegas in Nevada and we stayed at the Mirage.
THE MIRAGE
THE MIRAGE
VIVA LAS VEGAS!
Mom, I slept with Michael, in his bedroom.
Well Jordy, you are not to do that ever again!! Y'hear me??
Michael, Jordy is not to sleep over in your room, geddit?? We don't like it!
Pleeeaaase June, I'm not like that, I could never hurt a child.
Me and Jordy, we have a pure, honest, open and loving relationship.
But you are my real family. I love you all sooooo much.
In the Chandler household, many doubts were rising.
I get concerned about him being kidnapped or something, being around Jackson!
Or what about some other crazy motherfuckers that could come creeping out of the woodwork.
And what exactly is the relationship Jackson has with my son??
So I invited Mr Chandler to Neverland also.
Evan, I am not trying to steal your son or your family, sir?

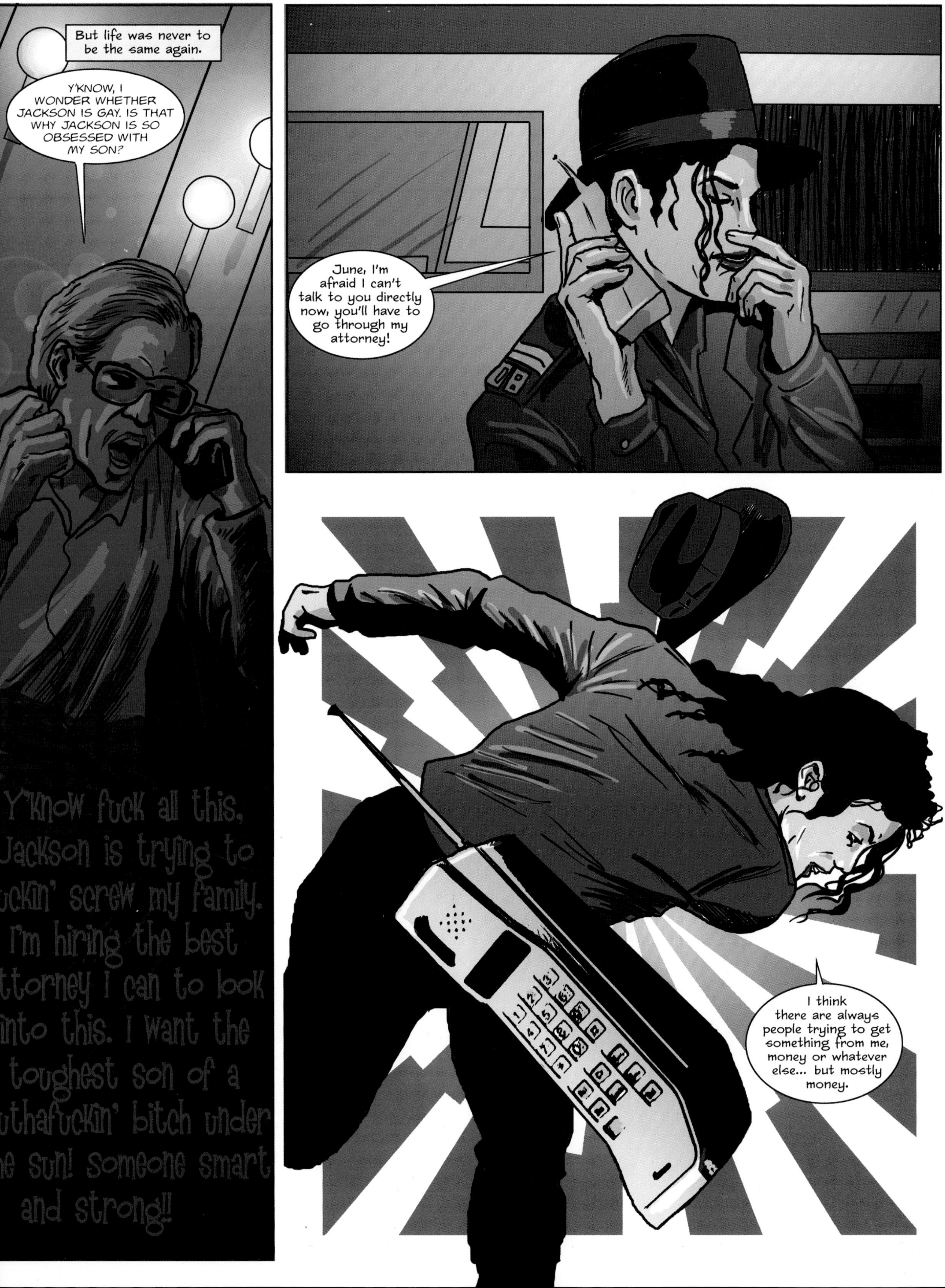
But life was never to be the same again.
Y'KNOW, I WONDER WHETHER JACKSON IS GAY. IS THAT WHY JACKSON IS SO OBSESSED WITH MY SON?
Y'know fuck all this, Jackson is trying to fuckin' screw my family. I'm hiring the best attorney I can to look into this. I want the toughest son of a muthafuckin' bitch under the sun! Someone smart and strong!!
June, I'm afraid I can't talk to you directly now, you'll have to go through my attorney!
I think there are always people trying to get something from me, money or whatever else... but mostly money.

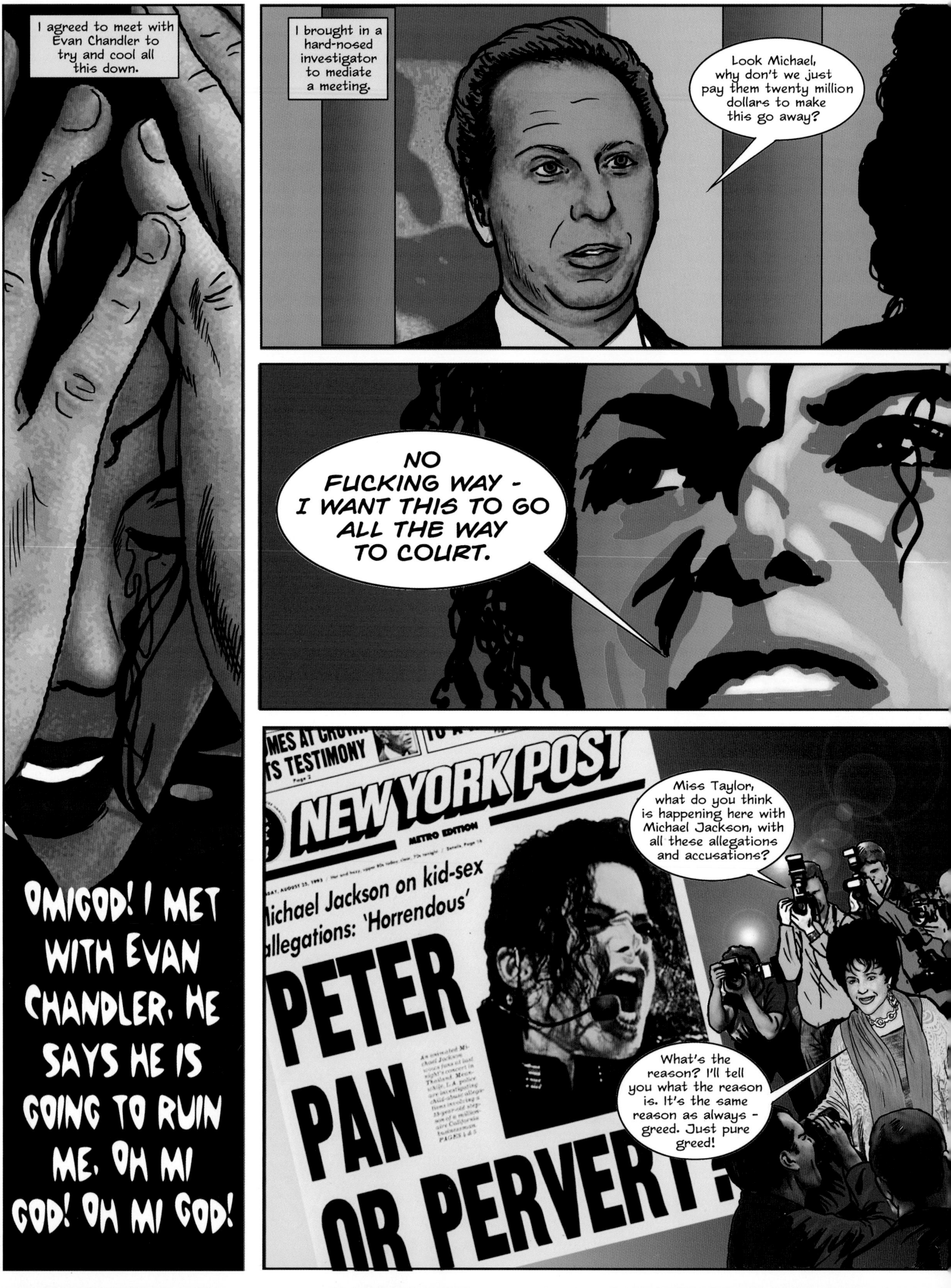
I agreed to meet with Evan Chandler to try and cool all this down.
OMIGOD! I MET WITH EVAN CHANDLER. HE SAYS HE IS GOING TO RUIN ME. OH MI GOD! OH MI GOD!
I brought in a hard-nosed investigator to mediate a meeting.
Look Michael, why don't we just pay them twenty million dollars to make this go away?
NO FUCKING WAY - I WANT THIS TO GO ALL THE WAY TO COURT.
NEW YORK POST
METRO EDITION
Michael Jackson on kid-sex allegations: 'Horrendous'
PETER PAN OR PERVERT
Miss Taylor, what do you think is happening here with Michael Jackson, with all these allegations and accusations?
What's the reason? I'll tell you what the reason is. It's the same reason as always - greed. Just pure greed!

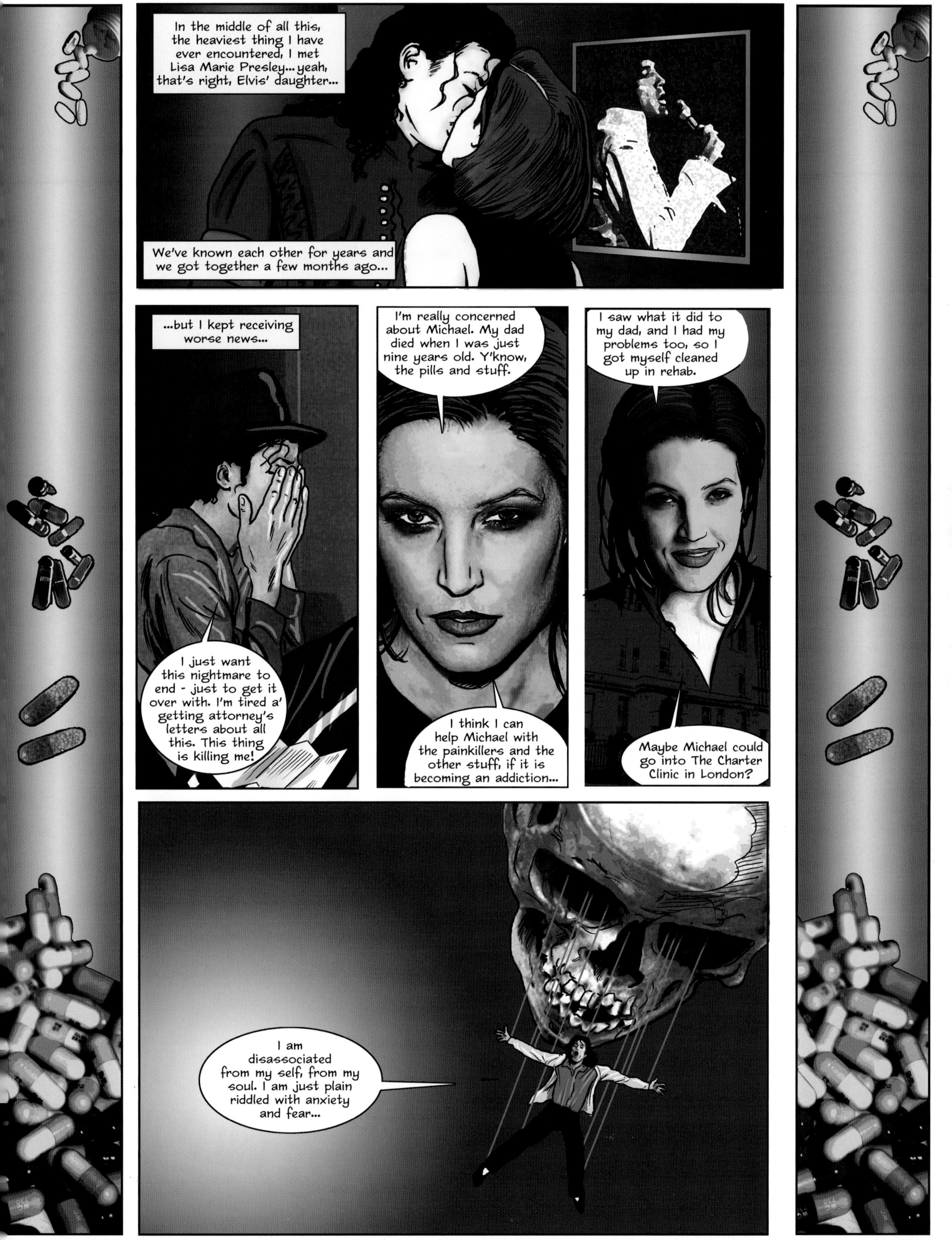
In the middle of all this, the heaviest thing I have ever encountered, I met Lisa Marie Presley... yeah, that's right, Elvis' daughter...
We've known each other for years and we got together a few months ago...
...but I kept receiving worse news...
I just want this nightmare to end - just to get it over with. I'm tired a' getting attorney's letters about all this. This thing is killing me!
I'm really concerned about Michael. My dad died when I was just nine years old. Y'know, the pills and stuff.
I think I can help Michael with the painkillers and the other stuff, if it is becoming an addiction...
I saw what it did to my dad, and I had my problems too, so I got myself cleaned up in rehab.
Maybe Michael could go into The Charter Clinic in London?
I am disassociated from my self, from my soul. I am just plain riddled with anxiety and fear...

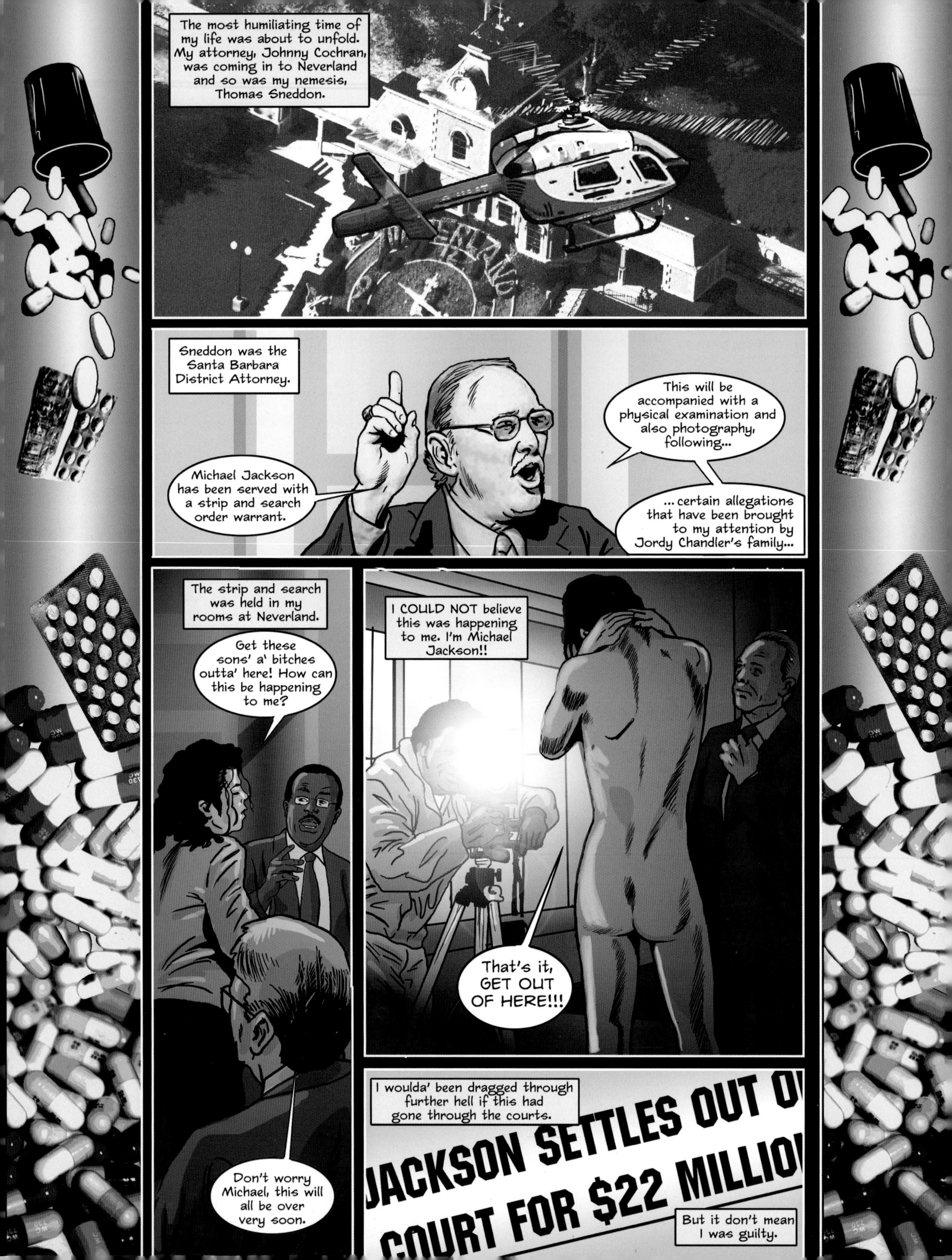
The most humiliating time of my life was about to unfold. My attorney, Johnny Cochran, was coming in to Neverland and so was my nemesis, Thomas Sneddon.
Sneddon was the Santa Barbara District Attorney.
Michael Jackson has been served with a strip and search order warrant.
This will be accompanied with a physical examination and also photography, following...
... certain allegations that have been brought to my attention by Jordy Chandler's family...
The strip and search was held in my rooms at Neverland.
Get these sons' a' bitches outta' here! How can this be happening to me?
Don't worry Michael, this will all be over very soon.
I COULD NOT believe this was happening to me. I'm Michael Jackson!!
That's it, GET OUT OF HERE!!!
I woulda' been dragged through further hell if this had gone through the courts.
JACKSON SETTLES OUT O
COURT FOR $22 MILLIO
But it don't mean I was guilty.

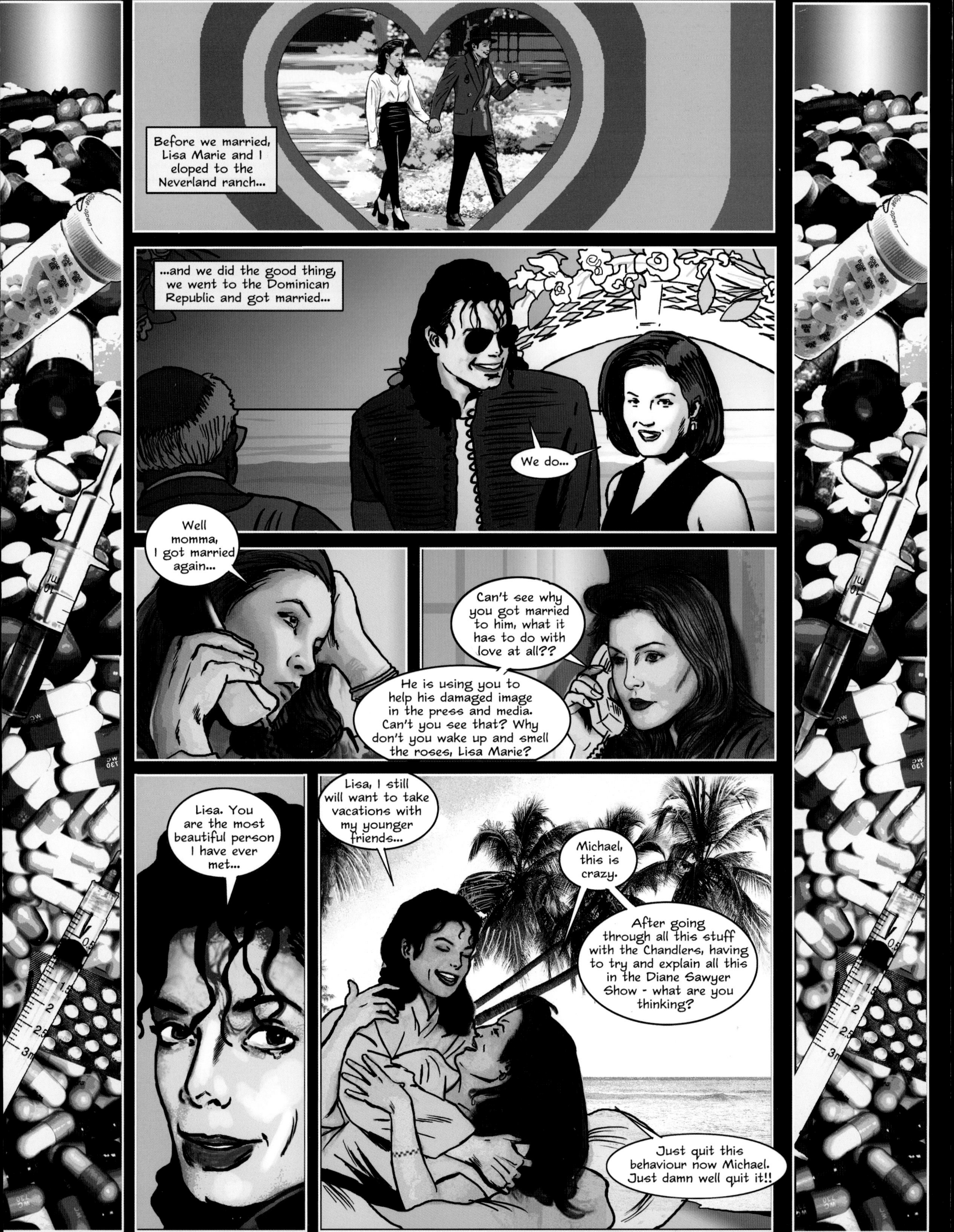
Before we married, Lisa Marie and I eloped to the Neverland ranch...
...and we did the good thing, we went to the Dominican Republic and got married...
We do...
Well momma, I got married again...
Can't see why you got married to him, what it has to do with love at all??
He is using you to help his damaged image in the press and media. Can't you see that? Why don't you wake up and smell the roses, Lisa Marie?
Lisa. You are the most beautiful person I have ever met...
Lisa, I still will want to take vacations with my younger friends...
Michael, this is crazy.
After going through all this stuff with the Chandlers, having to try and explain all this in the Diane Sawyer Show - what are you thinking?
Just quit this behaviour now Michael. Just damn well quit it!!

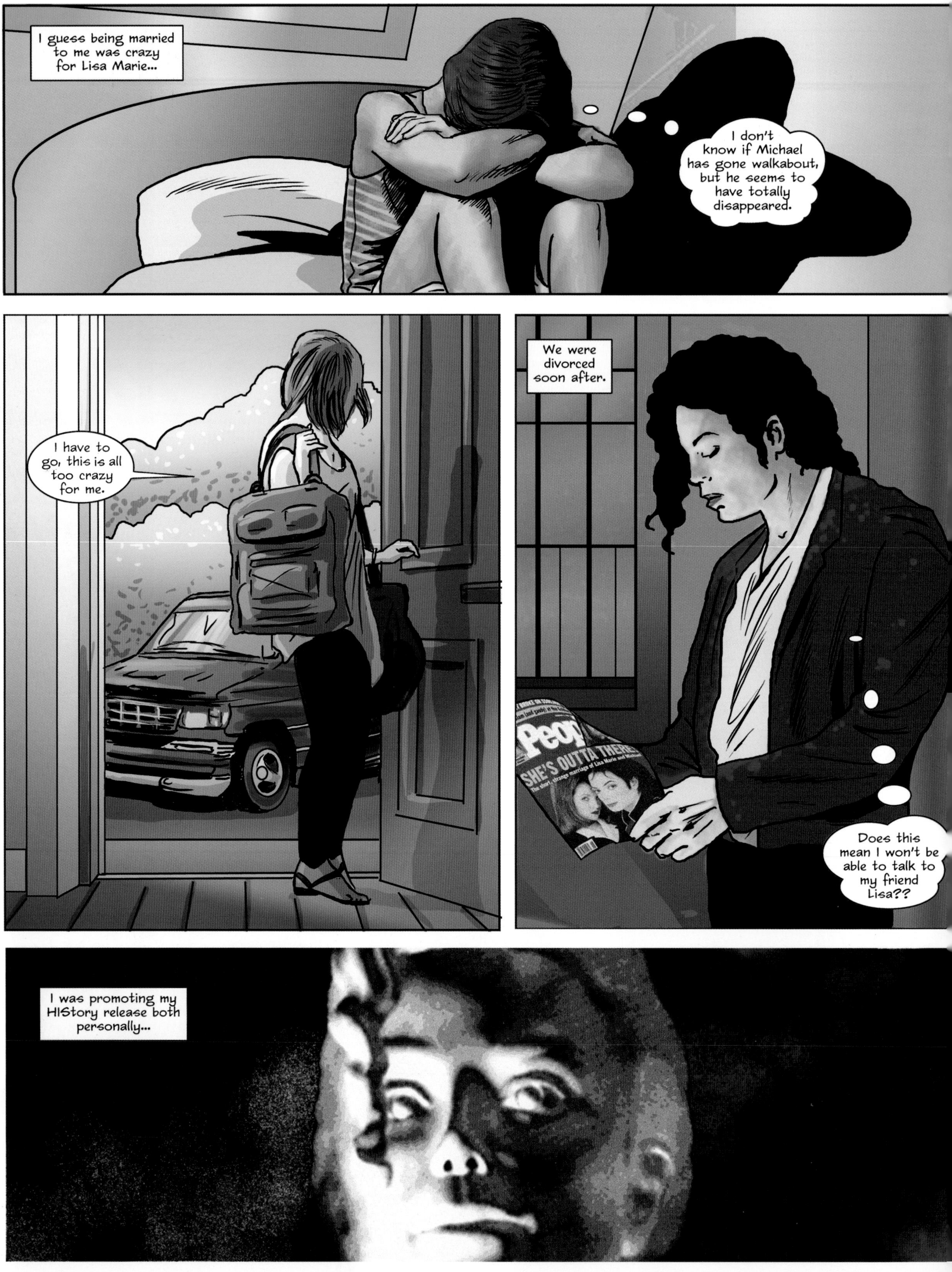
I guess being married to me was crazy for Lisa Marie...
I don't know if Michael has gone walkabout, but he seems to have totally disappeared.
I have to go, this is all too crazy for me.
We were divorced soon after.
People
SHE'S OUTTA THERE!
Does this mean I won't be able to talk to my friend Lisa??
I was promoting my HIStory release both personally...

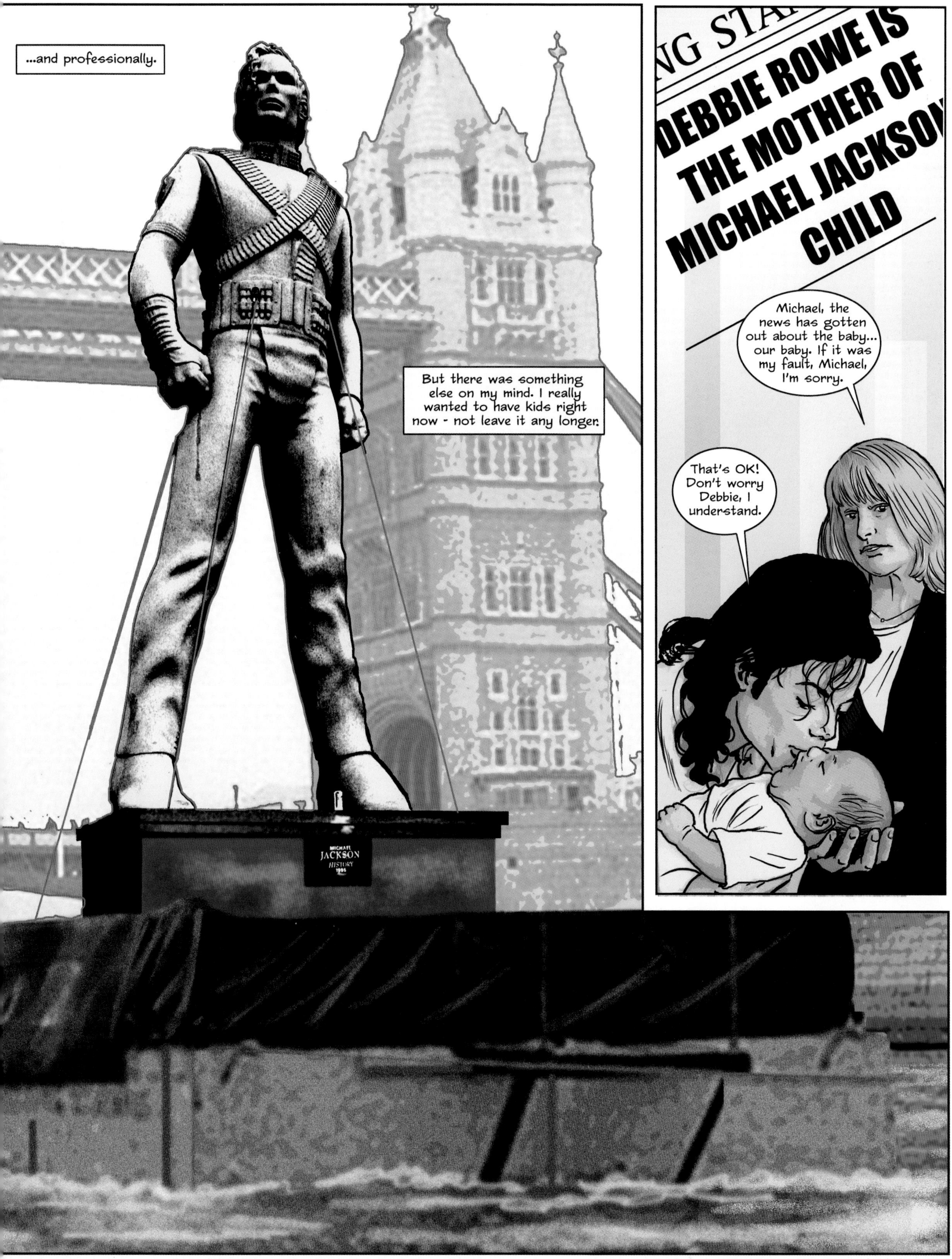
...and professionally.
But there was something else on my mind. I really wanted to have kids right now - not leave it any longer.
MICHAEL JACKSON HISTORY 1995
NG STA
DEBBIE ROWE IS THE MOTHER OF MICHAEL JACKSON CHILD
Michael, the news has gotten out about the baby... our baby. If it was my fault, Michael, I'm sorry.
That's OK! Don't worry Debbie, I understand.

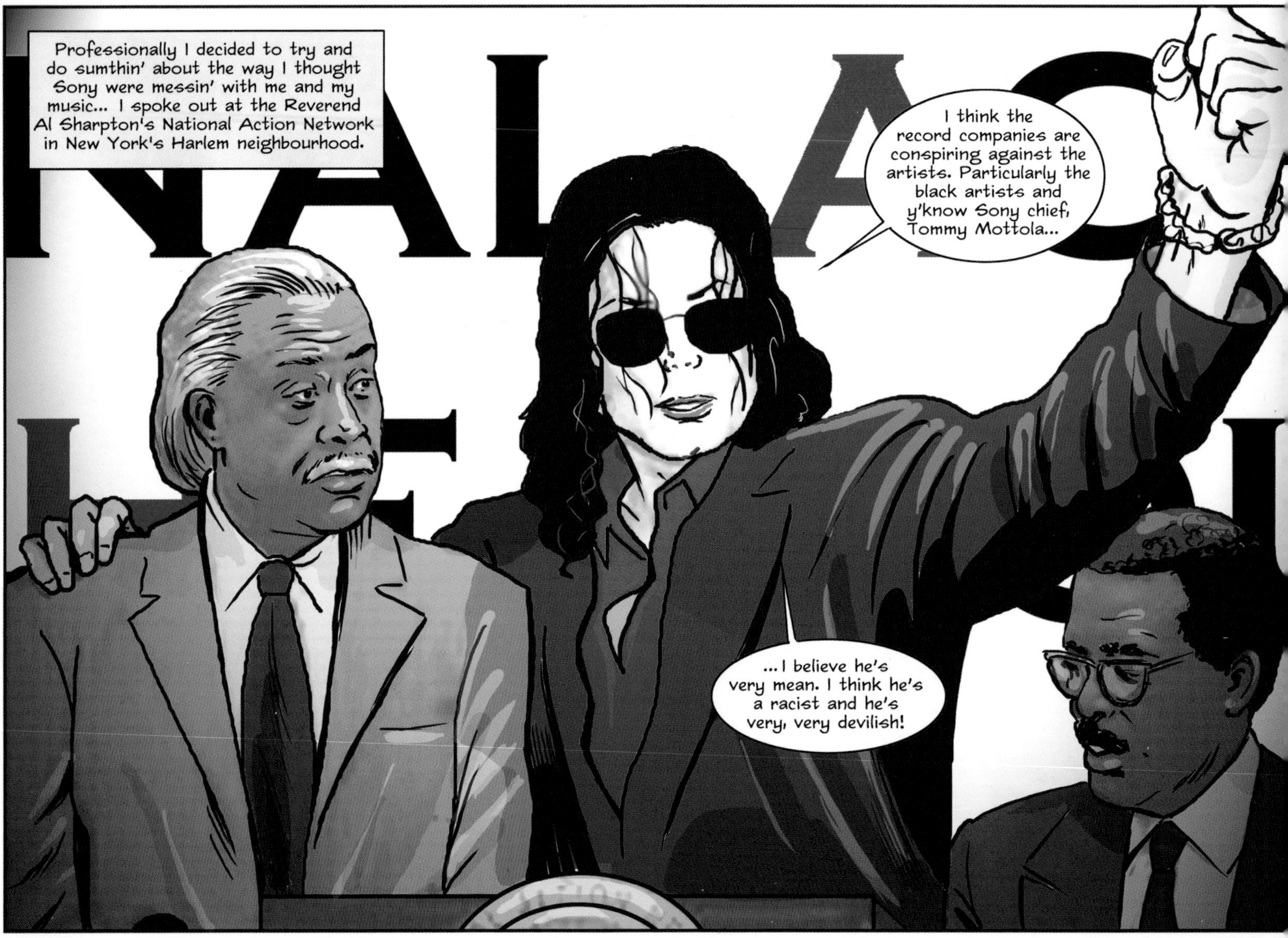
Professionally I decided to try and do sumthin' about the way I thought Sony were messin' with me and my music... I spoke out at the Reverend Al Sharpton's National Action Network in New York's Harlem neighbourhood.
I think the record companies are conspiring against the artists. Particularly the black artists and y'know Sony chief, Tommy Mottola...
...I believe he's very mean. I think he's a racist and he's very, very devilish!

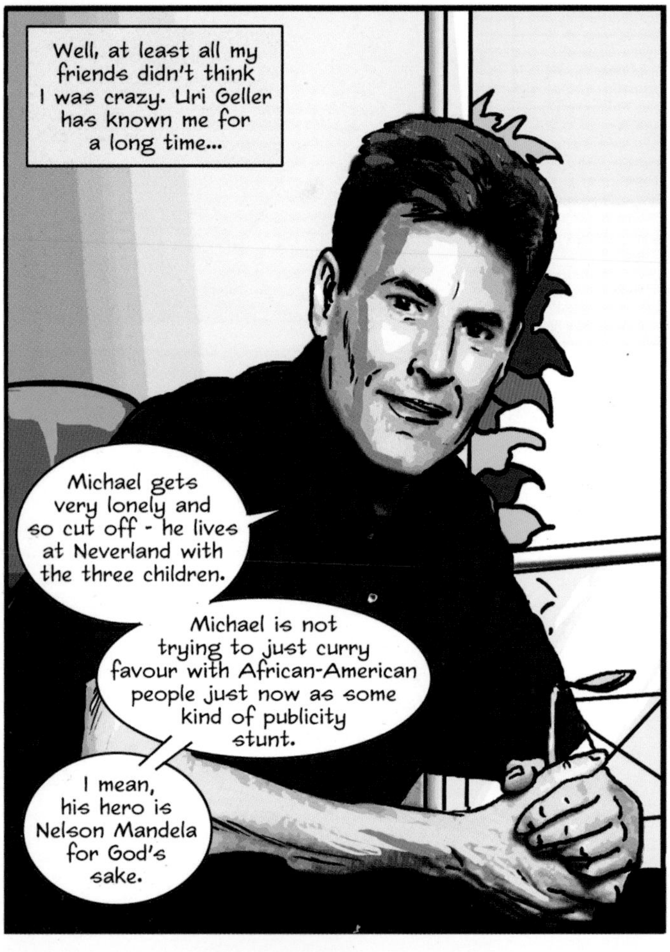
Well, at least all my friends didn't think I was crazy. Uri Geller has known me for a long time...
Michael gets very lonely and so cut off - he lives at Neverland with the three children.
Michael is not trying to just curry favour with African-American people just now as some kind of publicity stunt.
I mean, his hero is Nelson Mandela for God's sake.

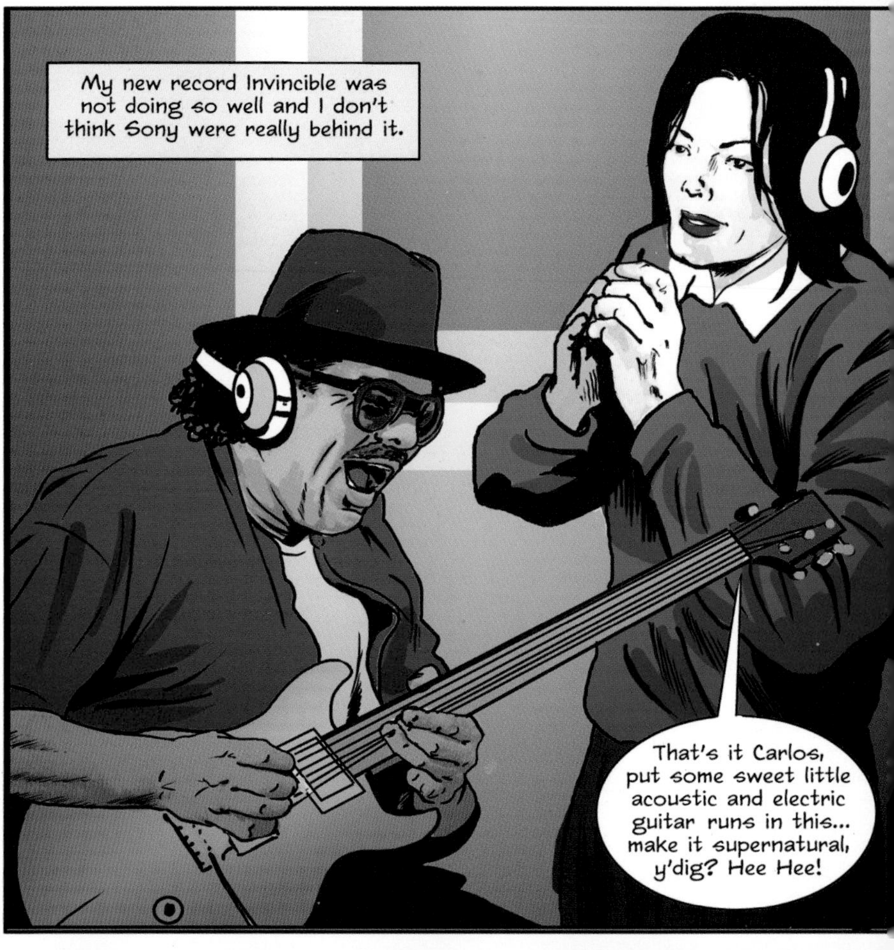
My new record Invincible was not doing so well and I don't think Sony were really behind it.
That's it Carlos, put some sweet little acoustic and electric guitar runs in this... make it supernatural, y'dig? Hee Hee!

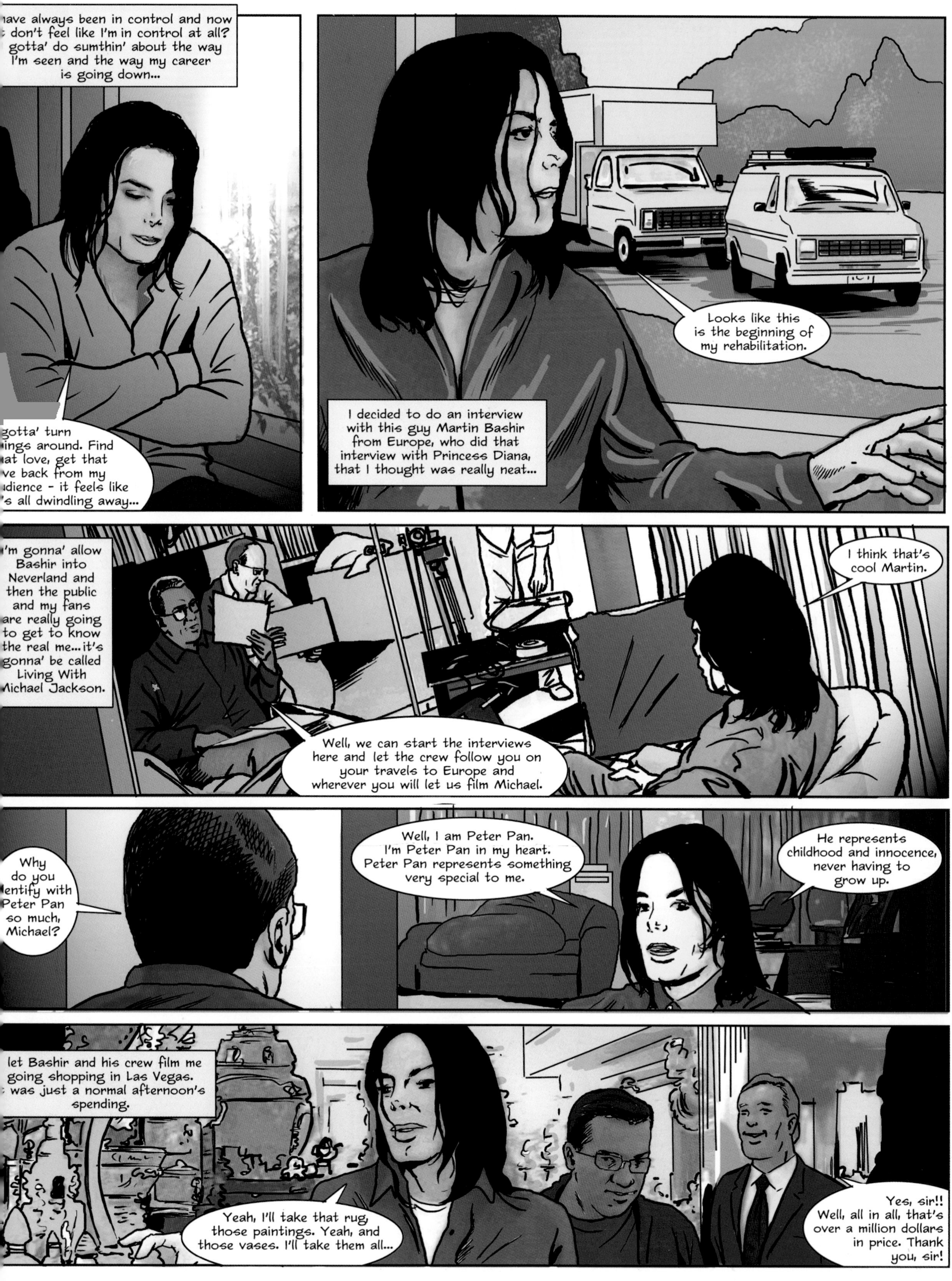
ave always been in control and now
don't feel like I'm in control at all?
gotta' do sumthin' about the way
I'm seen and the way my career
is going down...
gotta' turn
ings around. Find
at love, get that
e back from my
dience - it feels like
's all dwindling away...
I decided to do an interview with this guy Martin Bashir from Europe, who did that interview with Princess Diana, that I thought was really neat...
Looks like this is the beginning of my rehabilitation.
'm gonna' allow Bashir into Neverland and then the public and my fans are really going to get to know the real me... it's gonna' be called Living With Michael Jackson.
Well, we can start the interviews here and let the crew follow you on your travels to Europe and wherever you will let us film Michael.
I think that's cool Martin.
Why do you entify with Peter Pan so much, Michael?
Well, I am Peter Pan. I'm Peter Pan in my heart. Peter Pan represents something very special to me.
He represents childhood and innocence, never having to grow up.
let Bashir and his crew film me going shopping in Las Vegas. was just a normal afternoon's spending.
Yeah, I'll take that rug, those paintings. Yeah, and those vases. I'll take them all...
Yes, sir!! Well, all in all, that's over a million dollars in price. Thank you, sir!

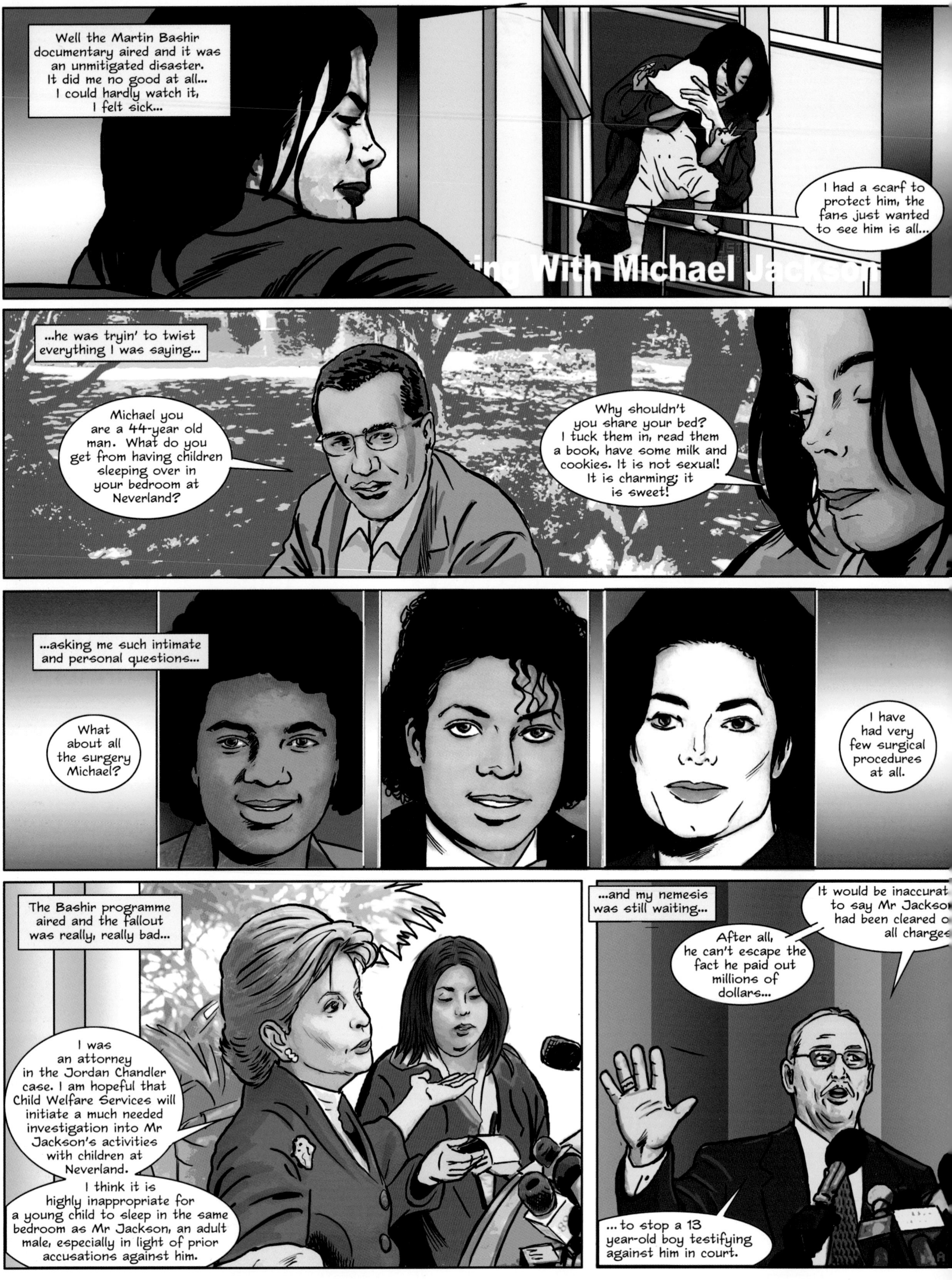

Well the Martin Bashir documentary aired and it was an unmitigated disaster. It did me no good at all... I could hardly watch it, I felt sick...
I had a scarf to protect him, the fans just wanted to see him is all...
ing With Michael Jackson
...he was tryin' to twist everything I was saying...
Michael you are a 44-year old man. What do you get from having children sleeping over in your bedroom at Neverland?
Why shouldn't you share your bed? I tuck them in, read them a book, have some milk and cookies. It is not sexual! It is charming; it is sweet!
...asking me such intimate and personal questions...
What about all the surgery Michael?
I have had very few surgical procedures at all.
The Bashir programme aired and the fallout was really, really bad...
I was an attorney in the Jordan Chandler case. I am hopeful that Child Welfare Services will initiate a much needed investigation into Mr Jackson's activities with children at Neverland.
I think it is highly inappropriate for a young child to sleep in the same bedroom as Mr Jackson, an adult male, especially in light of prior accusations against him.
...and my nemesis was still waiting...
It would be inaccurat to say Mr Jackso had been cleared o all charges
After all, he can't escape the fact he paid out millions of dollars...
...to stop a 13 year-old boy testifying against him in court.

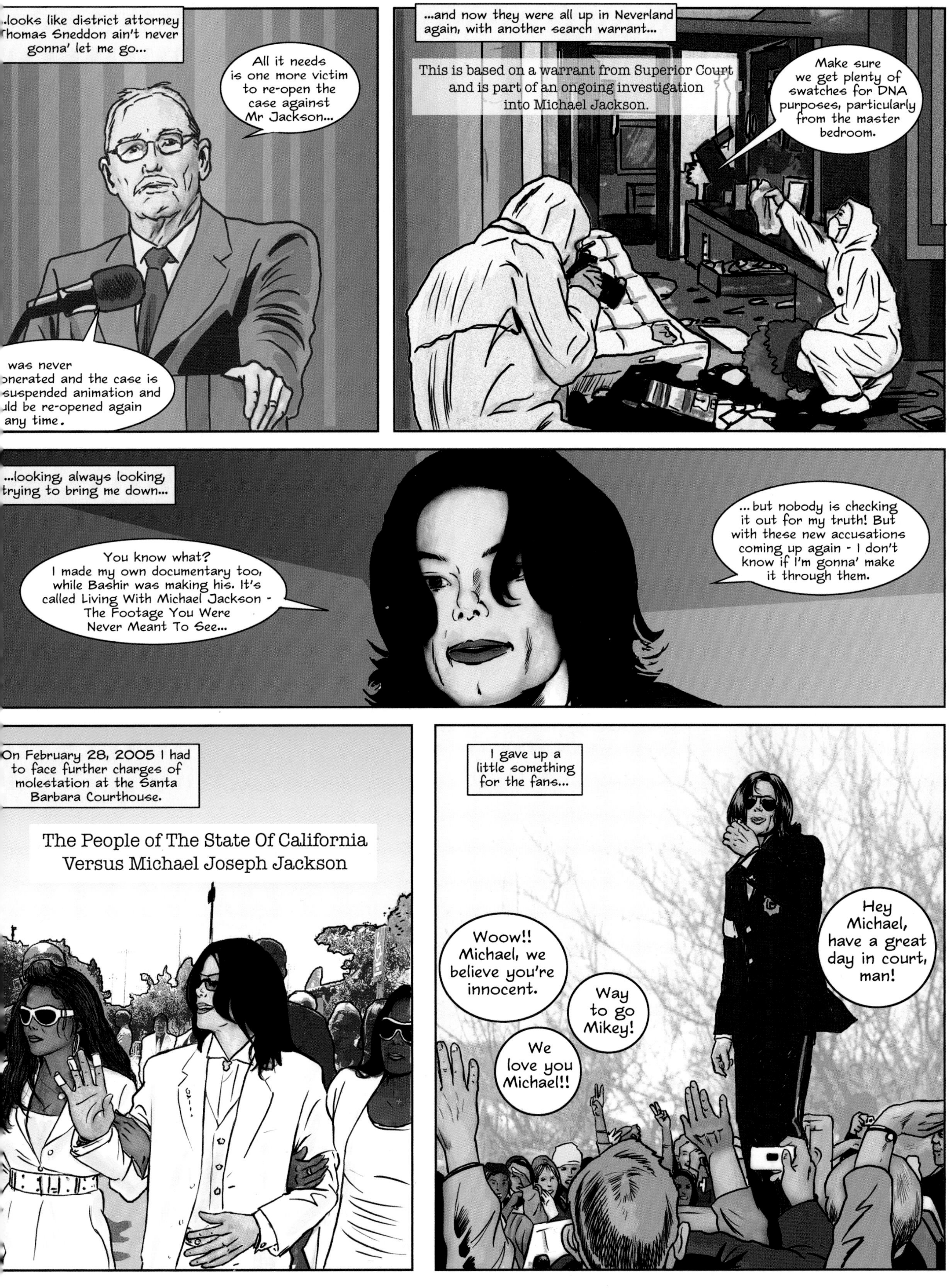
..looks like district attorney Thomas Sneddon ain't never gonna' let me go...
All it needs is one more victim to re-open the case against Mr Jackson...
was never onerated and the case is suspended animation and uld be re-opened again any time.
...and now they were all up in Neverland again, with another search warrant...
This is based on a warrant from Superior Court and is part of an ongoing investigation into Michael Jackson.
Make sure we get plenty of swatches for DNA purposes, particularly from the master bedroom.
...looking, always looking, trying to bring me down...
You know what? I made my own documentary too, while Bashir was making his. It's called Living With Michael Jackson - The Footage You Were Never Meant To See...
...but nobody is checking it out for my truth! But with these new accusations coming up again - I don't know if I'm gonna' make it through them.
On February 28, 2005 I had to face further charges of molestation at the Santa Barbara Courthouse.
The People of The State Of California Versus Michael Joseph Jackson
I gave up a little something for the fans...
Woow!! Michael, we believe you're innocent.
Way to go Mikey!
We love you Michael!!
Hey Michael, have a great day in court, man!

Inside the court things were much more serious... the trial dragged on...

Mr Jackson, you have here been accused of ten counts of molestation.

I am the presiding judge in this courtroom. My name is Rodney S Melville.

I believed in my people and my innocence...

My name is Thomas A. Mesereau Jr.

I am Mr Jackson's defence lawyer and I'm here to tell you these accusations are false...

... they are bogus and they never happened. These charges are fake, just silly!

We will prove that these children are tools and have been coached to make these accusations.

They had the perfect mark - the most vulnerable celebrity, the most known celebrity of all - Michael Jackson!

I started to ache all over my body; I was in such pain all the time. The pressure was killing me...

I am ordering your client, Mr Jackson, to return to this court...

... within one hour from this time!! Or I will have bail revoked immediately

...I feel so dizzy I can hardly stand up straight... but I got back there within the hour...

...and I still had some friends left...

Yes. Sir. My name is Macaulay Culkin. I have known Michael since I was a child.

He never molested me, he never touched me in any inappropriate sexual way at all.

These allegations are absolutely ridiculous.

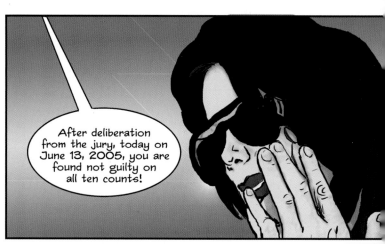

After deliberation from the jury, today on June 13, 2005, you are found not guilty on all ten counts!

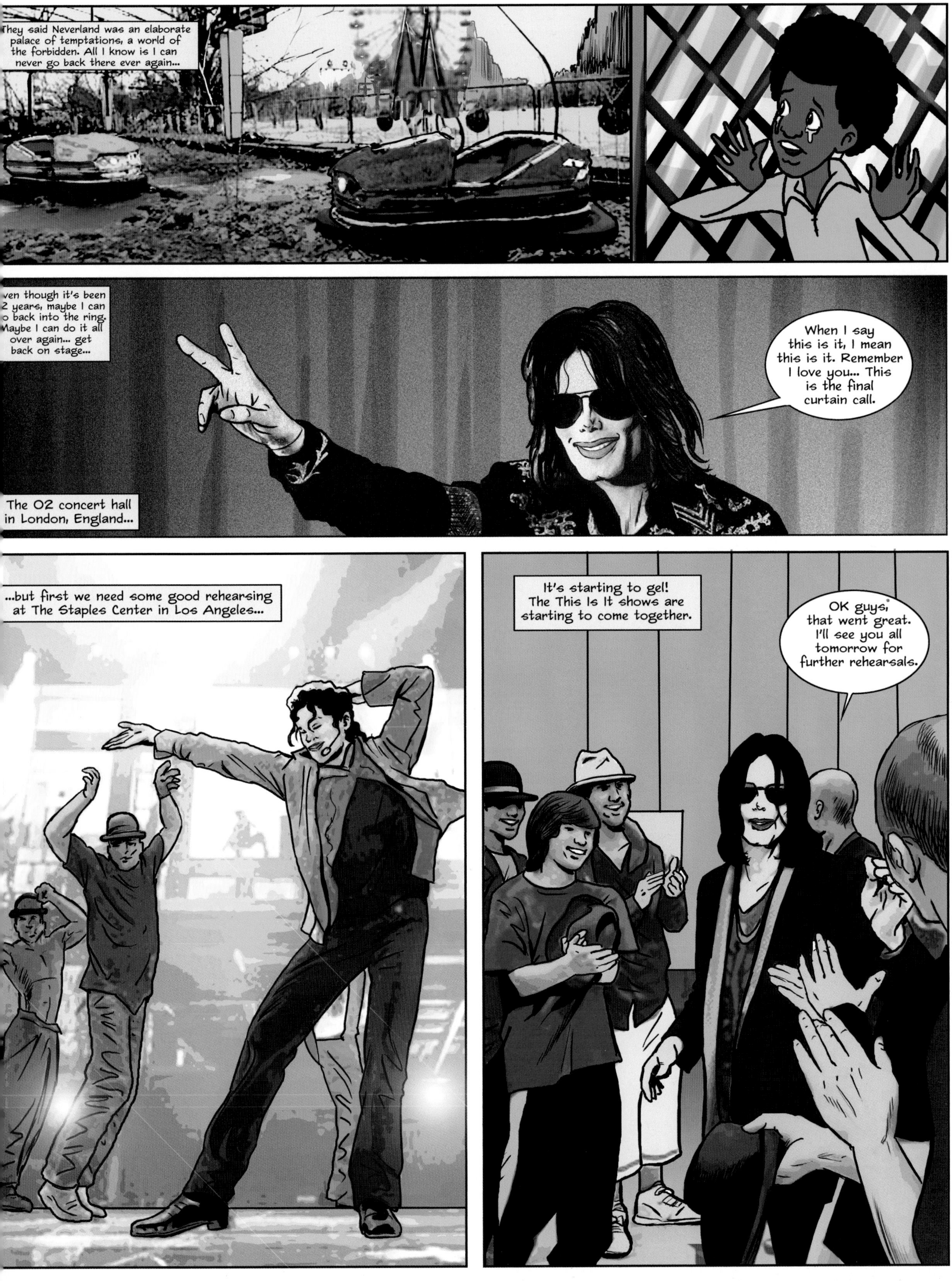
They said Neverland was an elaborate palace of temptations, a world of the forbidden. All I know is I can never go back there ever again...
ven though it's been 2 years, maybe I can o back into the ring. Maybe I can do it all over again... get back on stage...
When I say this is it, I mean this is it. Remember I love you... This is the final curtain call.
The O2 concert hall in London, England...
...but first we need some good rehearsing at The Staples Center in Los Angeles...
It's starting to gel! The This Is It shows are starting to come together.
OK guys, that went great. I'll see you all tomorrow for further rehearsals.

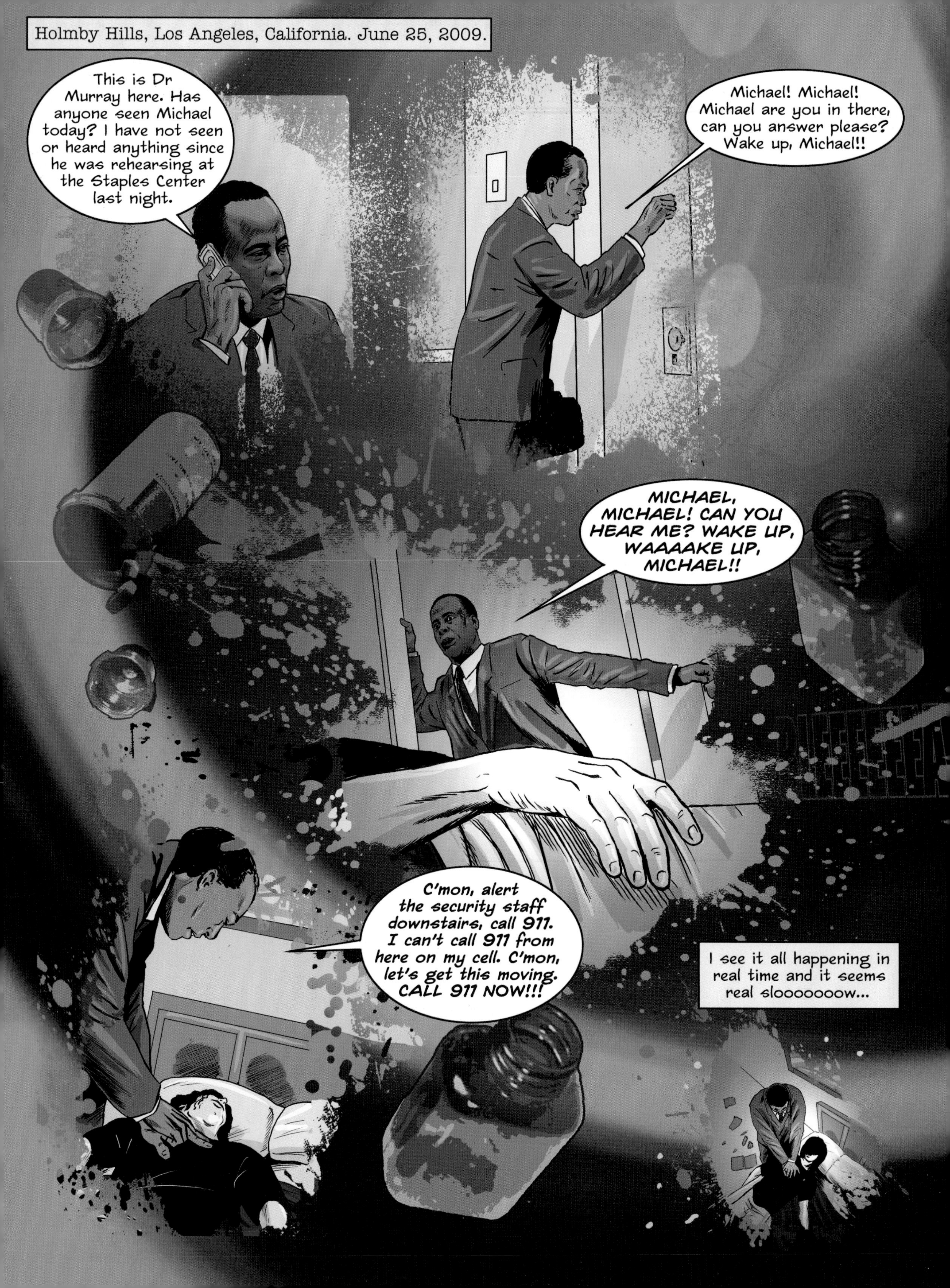
Holmby Hills, Los Angeles, California. June 25, 2009.
This is Dr Murray here. Has anyone seen Michael today? I have not seen or heard anything since he was rehearsing at the Staples Center last night.
Michael! Michael! Michael are you in there, can you answer please? Wake up, Michael!!
MICHAEL, MICHAEL! CAN YOU HEAR ME? WAKE UP, WAAAAKE UP, MICHAEL!!
C'mon, alert the security staff downstairs, call 911. I can't call 911 from here on my cell. C'mon, let's get this moving. CALL 911 NOW!!!
I see it all happening in real time and it seems real slooooooow...

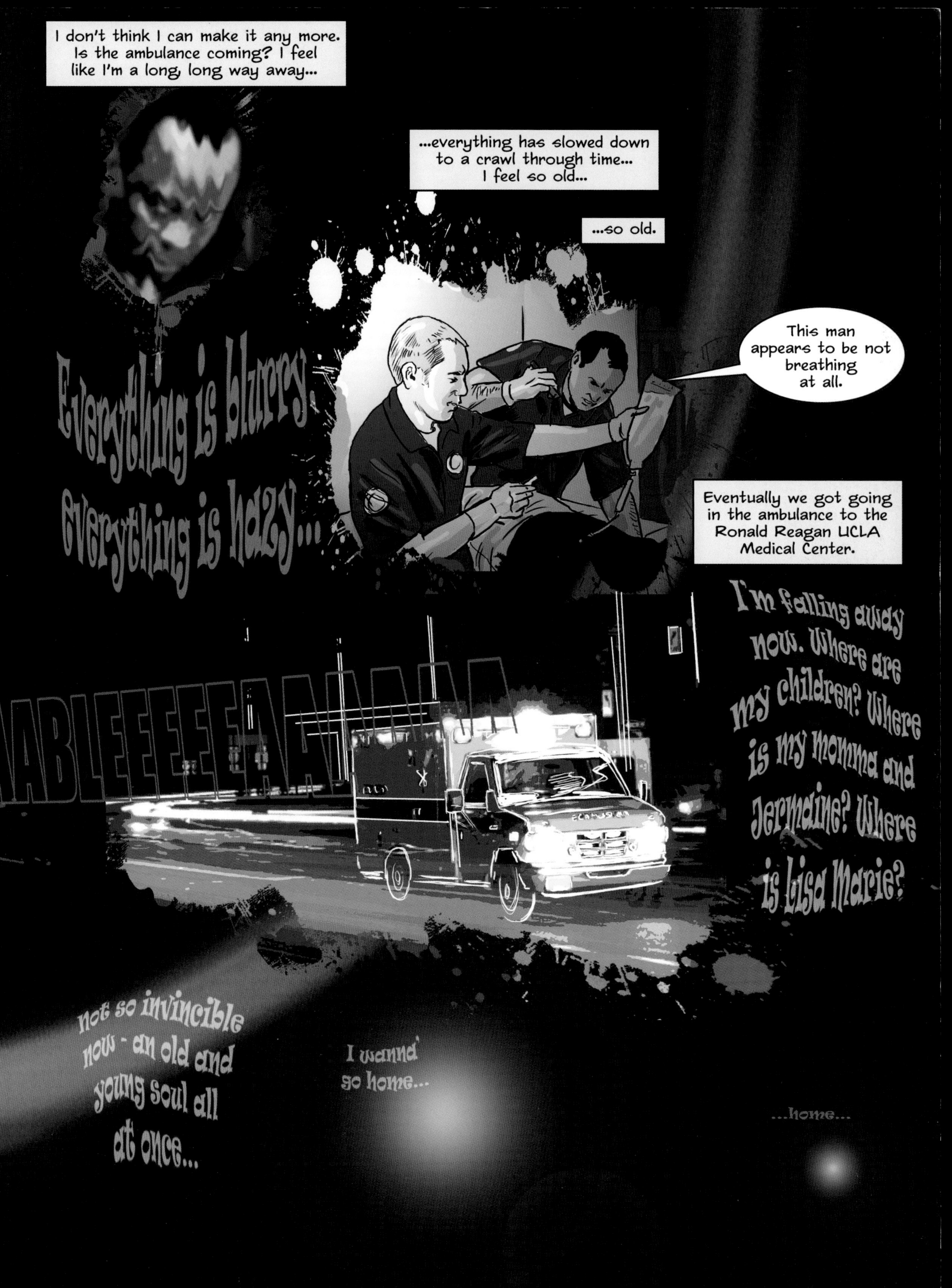
I don't think I can make it any more. Is the ambulance coming? I feel like I'm a long, long way away...
...everything has slowed down to a crawl through time... I feel so old...
...so old.
Everything is blurry, everything is hazy...
This man appears to be not breathing at all.
Eventually we got going in the ambulance to the Ronald Reagan UCLA Medical Center.
I'm falling away now. Where are my children? Where is my momma and Jermaine? Where is Lisa Marie?
not so invincible now - an old and young soul all at once...
I wanna go home...
...home...

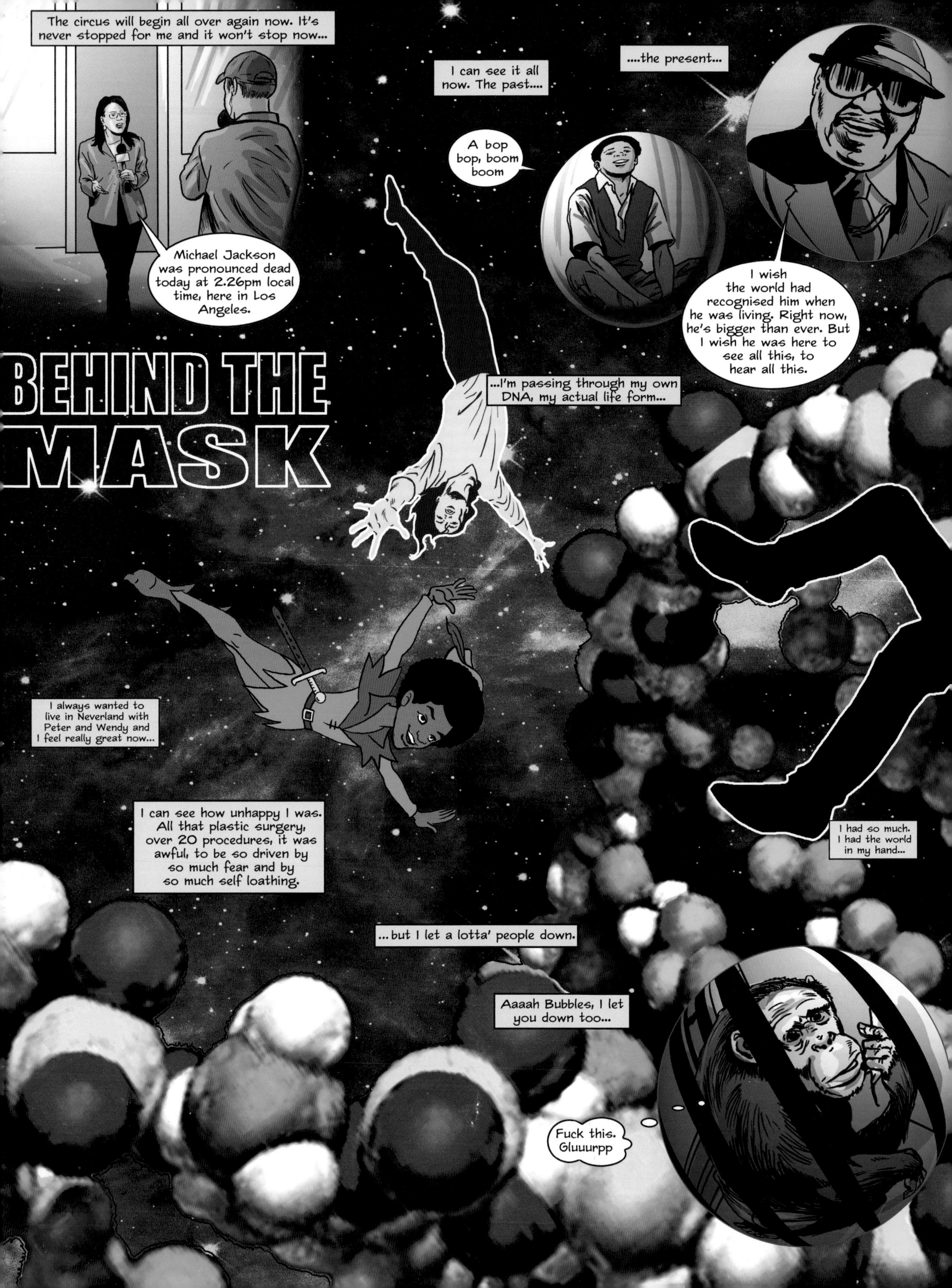
The circus will begin all over again now. It's never stopped for me and it won't stop now...
Michael Jackson was pronounced dead today at 2.26pm local time, here in Los Angeles.
BEHIND THE MASK
I can see it all now. The past....
A bop bop, boom boom
....the present...
I wish the world had recognised him when he was living. Right now, he's bigger than ever. But I wish he was here to see all this, to hear all this.
...I'm passing through my own DNA, my actual life form...
I always wanted to live in Neverland with Peter and Wendy and I feel really great now...
I can see how unhappy I was. All that plastic surgery, over 20 procedures, it was awful, to be so driven by so much fear and by so much self loathing.
I had so much. I had the world in my hand...
...but I let a lotta' people down.
Aaaah Bubbles, I let you down too...
Fuck this. Gluuurpp

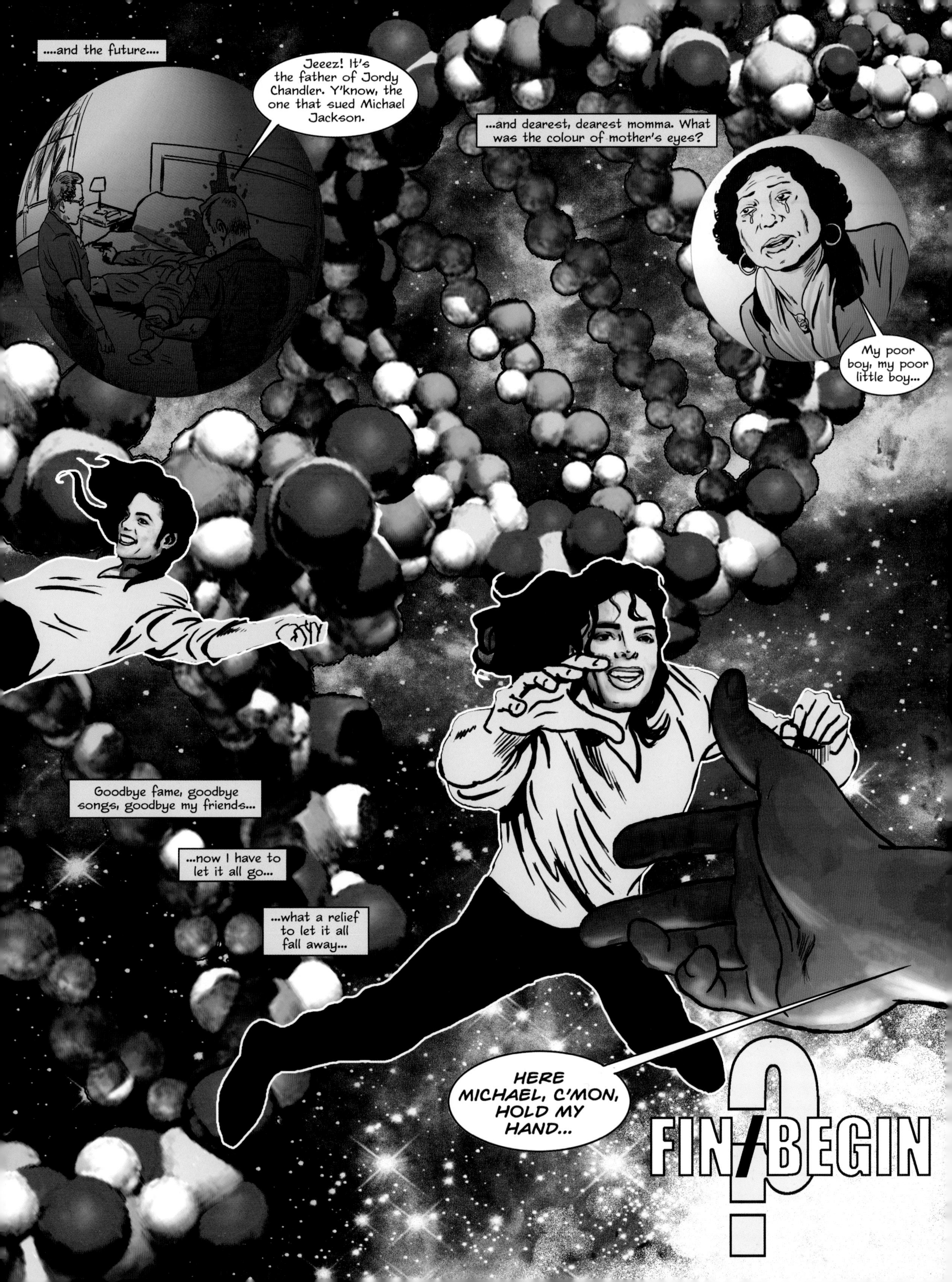

....and the future....
Jeeez! It's the father of Jordy Chandler. Y'know, the one that sued Michael Jackson.
...and dearest, dearest momma. What was the colour of mother's eyes?
My poor boy, my poor little boy...
Goodbye fame, goodbye songs, goodbye my friends...
...now I have to let it all go...
...what a relief to let it all fall away...
HERE MICHAEL, C'MON, HOLD MY HAND...
FIN/BEGIN
?

SKETCHBOOK

IT USUALLY GOES LIKE THIS:

"HEY BRI, LONG TIME NO SEE - WHAT'RE YOU WORKING ON THESE DAYS?"

"OH, I'M DRAWING A GRAPHIC NOVEL CALLED NEVERLAND. ABOUT MICHAEL JACKSON."

EYEBROWS RAISE AND THERE'S A SLIGHT INTAKE OF BREATH AS THEY PREPARE TO ASK THE QUESTION.

I'M SICK OF THE QUESTION. SINCE STARTING ON THE BOOK I GET ASKED THE QUESTION A LOT, SO I GET IN FIRST AND DEFLECT WITH A JOKE.

"AT LEAST I DON'T GET BORED DRAWING HIM - HIS FACE CHANGES EVERY COUPLE OF PAGES."

POLITE LAUGHTER, CHANGE OF SUBJECT, JOB DONE.

BUT AS TIME WENT ON, AND THE PAGES PILED UP, I BECAME A LITTLE ASHAMED OF SUCH A GLIB DISMISSAL OF WHAT, TO MICHAEL JACKSON, WAS A MAJOR SOURCE OF EMOTIONAL PAIN THROUGHOUT HIS LIFE.

IN HIS SCRIPT JIM (McCARTHY) HANDLES THE ISSUE WITH MORE SENSITIVITY, GIVING US A STREAM OF CONSCIOUSNESS TAKE ON EVENTS, VIA A CLASSIC, UNRELIABLE NARRATOR - A LA SUNSET BOULEVARD - IN JACKSON HIMSELF. JIM MANAGES TO TEASE OUT A PORTRAIT OF A BELIEVABLY REAL PERSON FROM THE TANGLE OF PUBLICITY, TABLOID HEADLINES, LITIGATION AND INNUENDO.

EARLY ON WE DECIDED THAT WE WEREN'T GOING TO GO FOR A STRAIGHT "DOCUMENTARY" FEEL WITH OUR BOOK, SO YOU'LL FIND PASSAGES THAT ARE IMPRESSIONISTIC, FLIGHTS OF

FANCY - EVEN A COUPLE OF FLAT-OUT LIES. THAT SHOT OF THE DRIVEWAY UP TO PAUL McCARTNEY'S HOUSE? THAT'S NOT WHAT THE LOVABLE MOP-TOP'S DRIVEWAY REALLY LOOKS LIKE. I KNOW, BUT I'LL NEVER TELL. THE LAWYERS WOULDN'T LET ME ANYWAY.

AS FOR THE ART ITSELF, WHAT CAN I TELL YOU? UM, NOT MUCH, REALLY. TELL YOU WHAT, TAKE A SECOND AND FLICK THROUGH THE BOOK AGAIN. I'LL WAIT.

DONE? GOOD. NOW YOU KNOW AS MUCH AS I DO.

THE TECHNICAL STUFF? OH OKAY, BUT I WARN YOU, IT'S NOT EXACTLY A THRILLING READ. IT'S A FOUR-STEP PROCESS: READ THE SCRIPT; DRAW THE FIRST PAGE; SCAN IT INTO A MAC AND MESS ABOUT WITH IT UNTIL IT'S PRESENTABLE; RINSE AND REPEAT UNTIL DONE AND THE VOICES IN YOUR HEAD STOP SCREAMING. ONLY JOKING - THEY NEVER STOP SCREAMING. ALWAYS WITH THE SCREAMING.

YOU CAN SEE, ON THESE FEW PAGES, SOME OF THE COVER ROUGHS THAT WEREN'T USED. AFTER ALL THAT WORK, WE ENDED UP USING THE ORIGINAL IDEA, WITH SOME MINOR TWEAKS, WHICH ISN'T MUCH OF A SURPRISE AS YOU TEND TO SUBMIT YOUR BEST SHOT FIRST. STILL, I DO HAVE A LIKING FOR THE BUBBLES AND AEROPLANE IDEA. EXCEPT IDEALLY BUBBLES (WHO, INCIDENTALLY, GETS THE BEST LINE OF DIALOGUE IN THE BOOK) WOULD BE A GORILLA.

ALSO INCLUDED HERE IS MY ORIGINAL SAMPLE IMAGE, WHICH THE EAGLE-EYED AMONG YOU MAY HAVE NOTICED DOES MAKE AN APPEARANCE ELSEWHERE IN THE BOOK, IN A SOMEWHAT ALTERED FORM.

THAT'S ABOUT IT, I THINK. MY WORK HERE IS DONE.

SO BYE, SAFE HOME NOW, AND SEE YOU IN THE FUNNY PAGES.

BRIAN WILLIAMSON

DECEMBER 2011

OH, THE QUESTION?

OKAY THEN, FOR WHAT IT'S WORTH - NO, I DON'T THINK HE DID.

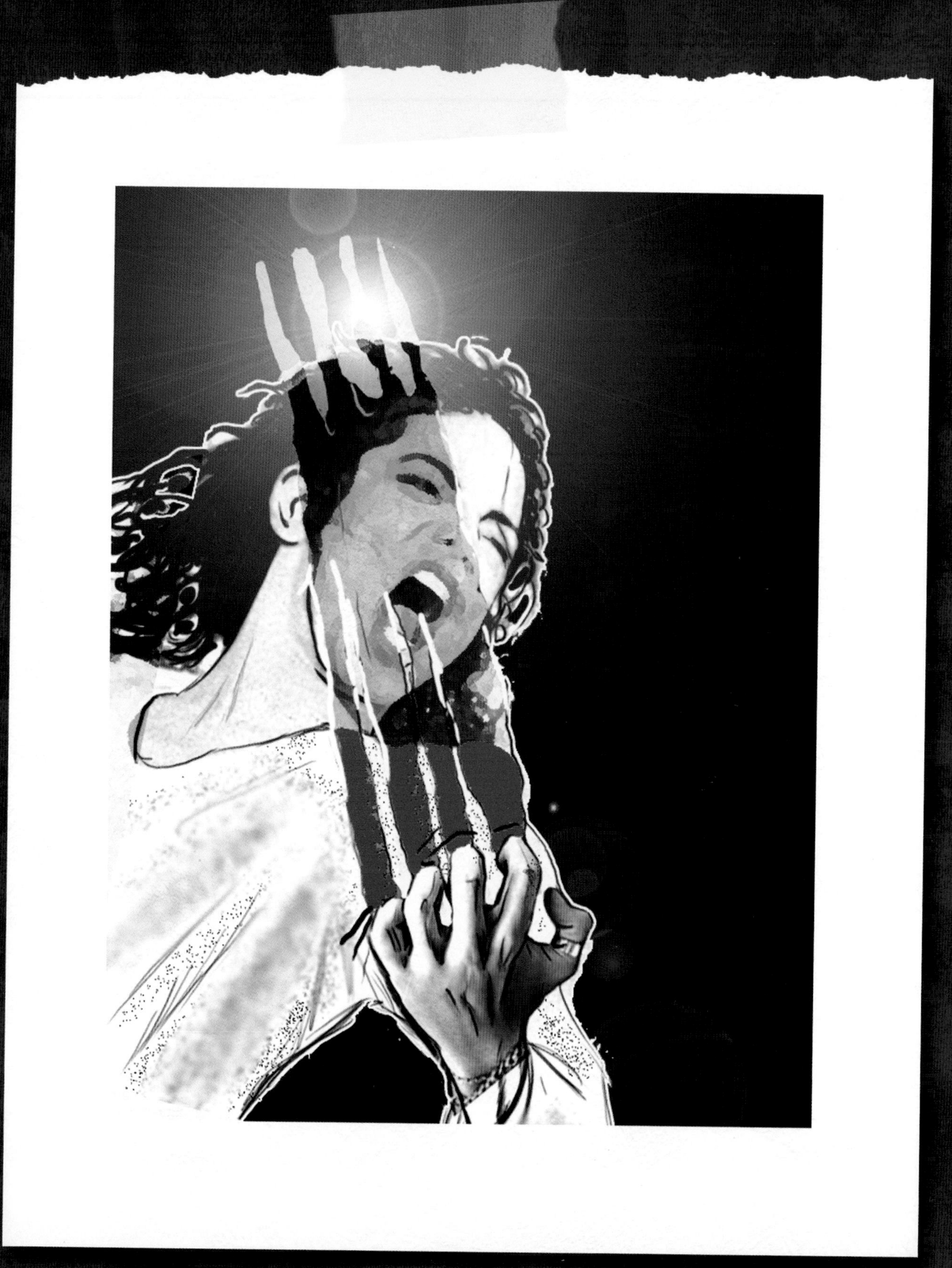

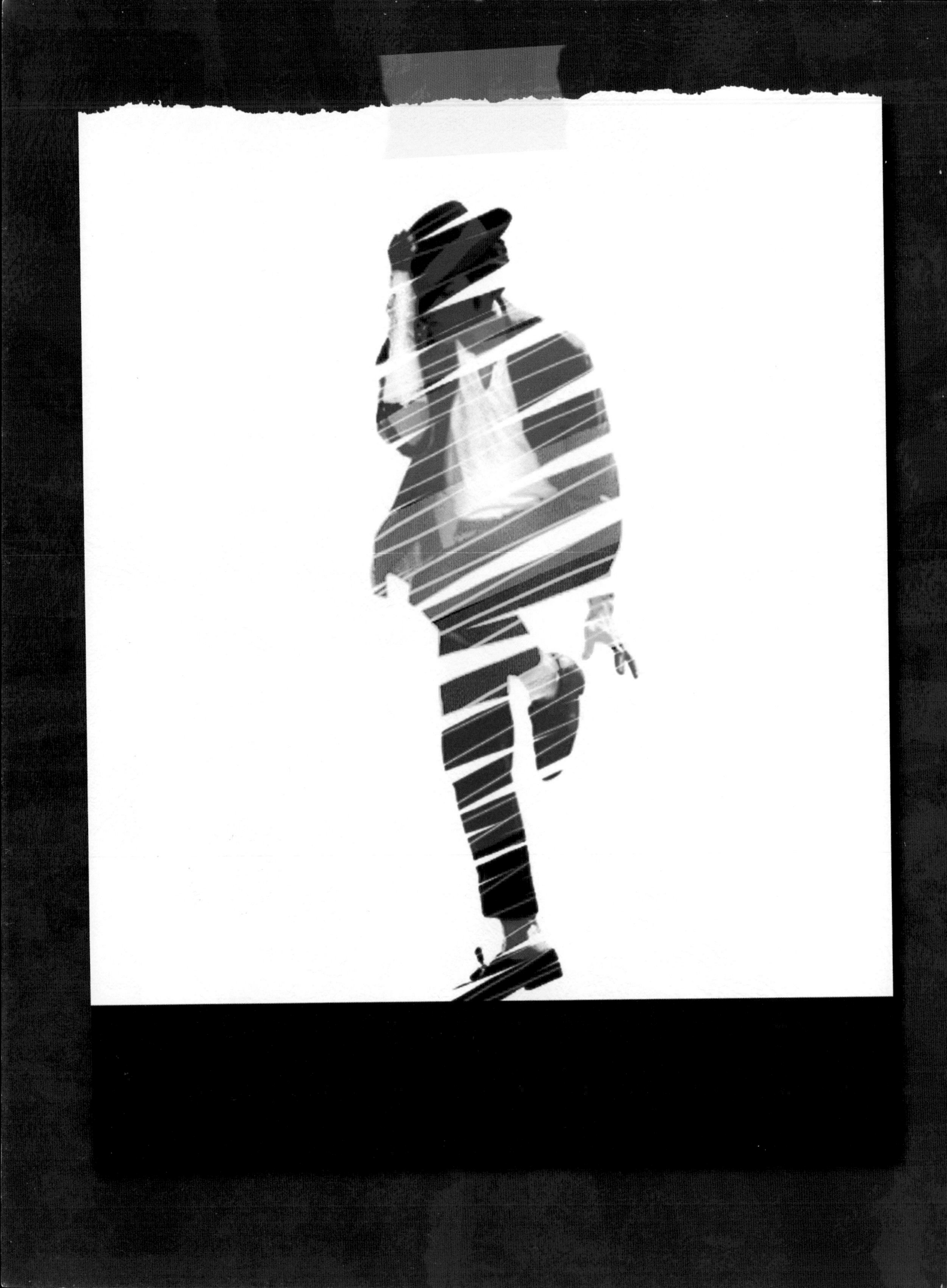

Also available from OMNIBUS PRESS...

GODSPEED
THE KURT COBAIN GRAPHIC
PARENTAL ADVISORY EXPLICIT CONTENTS
Flameboy
barnaby Legg . Jim mcCarthy . Flameboy

OP53867
978.1.84938.699.9
£9.95

Sex PistOLs
The Graphic NOVEL
written by
Jim McCarthY
illustrated by
steve ParkHouse
PARENTAL ADVISORY EXPLICIT CONTENTS

OP5434
978.1.78038.178.
£9.9

THE BEATLES GRAPHIC
HERVÉ BOURHIS

OP54296
978.1.78038.1565
£16.95

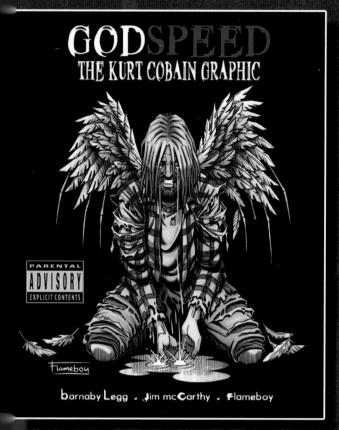

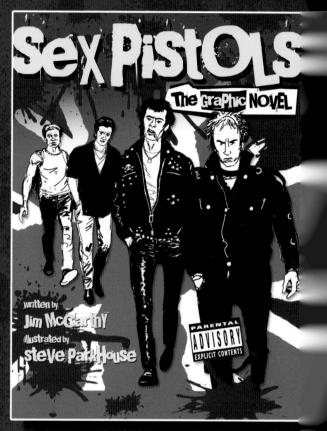

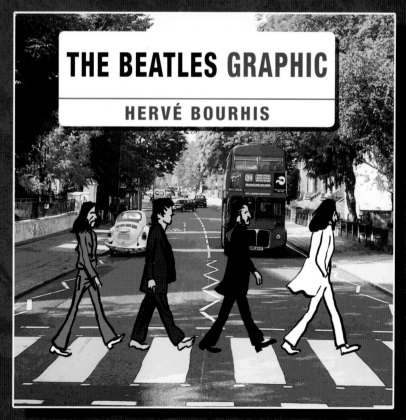